IT HAPPENED TO ME

Series Editor: Arlene Hirschfelder

Books in the It Happened to Me series are designed for inquisitive teens digging for answers about certain illnesses, social issues, or lifestyle interests. Whether you are deep into your teen years or just entering them, these books are gold mines of up-to-date information, riveting teen views, and great visuals to help you figure out stuff. Besides special boxes highlighting singular facts, each book is enhanced with the latest reading lists, websites, and an index. Perfect for browsing, there are loads of expert information by acclaimed writers to help parents, guardians, and librarians understand teen illness, tough situations, and lifestyle choices.

1. *Epilepsy: The Ultimate Teen Guide,* by Kathlyn Gay and Sean McGarrahan, 2002.
2. *Stress Relief: The Ultimate Teen Guide,* by Mark Powell, 2002.
3. *Learning Disabilities: The Ultimate Teen Guide,* by Penny Hutchins Paquette and Cheryl Gerson Tuttle, 2003.
4. *Making Sexual Decisions: The Ultimate Teen Guide,* by L. Kris Gowen, 2003.
5. *Asthma: The Ultimate Teen Guide,* by Penny Hutchins Paquette, 2003.
6. *Cultural Diversity-Conflicts and Challenges: The Ultimate Teen Guide,* by Kathlyn Gay, 2003.
7. *Diabetes: The Ultimate Teen Guide,* by Katherine J. Moran, 2004.
8. *When Will I Stop Hurting? Teens, Loss, and Grief: The Ultimate Teen Guide to Dealing with Grief,* by Ed Myers, 2004.
9. *Volunteering: The Ultimate Teen Guide,* by Kathlyn Gay, 2004.
10. *Organ Transplants—A Survival Guide for the Entire Family: The Ultimate Teen Guide,* by Tina P. Schwartz, 2005.
11. *Medications: The Ultimate Teen Guide,* by Cheryl Gerson Tuttle, 2005.
12. *Image and Identity—Becoming the Person You Are: The Ultimate Teen Guide,* by L. Kris Gowen and Molly C. McKenna, 2005.
13. *Apprenticeship: The Ultimate Teen Guide,* by Penny Hutchins Paquette, 2005.
14. *Cystic Fibrosis: The Ultimate Teen Guide,* by Melanie Ann Apel, 2006.
15. *Religion and Spirituality in America: The Ultimate Teen Guide,* by Kathlyn Gay, 2006.
16. *Gender Identity: The Ultimate Teen Guide,* by Cynthia L. Winfield, 2007.

ADOPTED

THE ULTIMATE TEEN GUIDE

REVISED EDITION

SUZANNE BUCKINGHAM SLADE

IT HAPPENED TO ME, NO. 34

THE SCARECROW PRESS, INC.
Lanham • Toronto • Plymouth, UK
2013

Published by Scarecrow Press, Inc.
A wholly owned subsidary of The Rowman & Littlefield Publishing Group, Inc.
4501 Forbes Boulevard, Suite 200, Lanham, Maryland 20706
www.rowman.com

10 Thornbury Road, Plymouth PL6 7PP, United Kingdom

British Library Cataloguing in Publication Information Available

Library of Congress Cataloging-in-Publication Data

Slade, Suzanne.
   Adopted : the ultimate teen guide / Suzanne Buckingham Slade. — Rev. ed.
      p. cm. — (It happened to me ; no. 34)
   Includes bibliographical references and index.
   ISBN 978-0-8108-8568-4 (cloth : alk. paper) — ISBN 978-0-8108-8569-1 (ebook)
   1. Adoption—United States. 2. Adoption. I. Title.
   HV875.55.S61 2013
   362.7340973—dc23

                                                          2012033949

∞™ The paper used in this publication meets the minimum requirements of American National Standard for Information Sciences—Permanence of Paper for Printed Library Materials, ANSI/NISO Z39.48-1992. Printed in the United States of America.

*With much love to my daughter, Christina,
and her birth mother, Christy*

Contents

Acknowledgments

This book reflects the effort and generosity of many. It is my privilege to express with words, although they will not be adequate, my gratitude to those who helped create this valuable resource for adopted teens.

First, I want to thank the adopted individuals (there were eighteen in all) who generously shared their personal stories and bravely explored their feelings about their own adoptions. Alanna, Allison, Andrew, Benjamin, Billy, Bryant, Derrico, Emily, Faith, Hope, Jonathan, Kamal, Liana, Lisa, Michael, Reva, Sarah, and Sasha—I enjoyed getting to know each one of you. Your courage inspired me, your energy sustained me, your faith encouraged me, and I know the stories of your adoption experiences will do the same for the teens who read them.

To the adoption professionals who kindly contributed their time and expertise, I cannot thank you enough. I know many teens will benefit from the timely and practical advice gained from your many years of experience in the adoption field. I am deeply indebted to each of you—Ms. Kathleen Morrison, Ms. Hollee McGinnis, Ms. Judy Stigger, Ms. Jenny Spinner, Ms. Ruth Mark, Ms. Barbara Hayes, Ms. Katrina Carlisle, and Ms. Diane Riggs.

My warm appreciation to the birth mothers who graciously shared their stories of sacrifice, courage, and love—Jamie, Beth, Sheila, and Mary. I am grateful to have met each of you. Your kindness warms my heart. And to the adoptive parents—Bill, Donna, Fred, and Patricia—who participated in and supported this project, I am indebted to you as well. And a very special thank you to Patricia Evans for coming alongside me and providing invaluable editorial insights.

I also thank Ms. Katy Robinson and Ms. Keiko Kasza, two excellent authors who shared their stories and thoughts on adoption. I wish to acknowledge their wonderful books, *A Single Square Picture* and *A Mother for Choco,* which are an inspiration to adopted teens everywhere.

With sincere gratitude I also express my thanks to the artists (each of whom has a special connection to adoption) for bringing their heart, energy, and talent to this book. Dr. Christopher Papile's cartoons so aptly convey thoughts and ideas in a way words simply cannot—I appreciate his passion for and work in the adoption field. Mary Sandage's art added so much depth to this book, and I could feel love for her birth daughter in each of her drawings. I am deeply grateful to Odelia Witt, not only for her skillful artwork (thirteen of her drawings appear in the book), but also for her friendship.

And many thanks to my photographer, Chris Washburn, for capturing the faces and lives of many adopted teens and their parents, and for sharing his design skills for the cover.

Finally, I am grateful to my husband of twenty years, Mike, who unselfishly supports my writing and encouraged me for the past two years as I completed this project. I love you.

Introduction: Is This for Real?

Adoption is very special to me. My first child, Christina, came into my life when she was only three days old as the result of the loving, caring, and unselfish decision of her wonderful birth mother and family. Through adoption, I became "Mom" and was given the privilege of raising the sweetest and most beautiful baby I had ever seen.

I think of adoption as a gift—an extraordinary gift inspired by love. While most gifts are given to only one person, there are many who actually receive this very special gift. A family receives a child. A child receives a family. And the child and parents are united for life, for better or worse, as a result of the wonderful and mysterious gift called adoption. While the birth mother is the giver of these gifts, in an adoption done right, she also receives peace and the future she longs for her child to have.

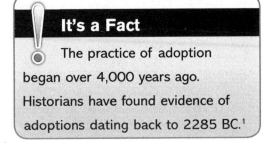

It's a Fact

The practice of adoption began over 4,000 years ago. Historians have found evidence of adoptions dating back to 2285 BC.[1]

I've heard some people say adoption is like a triangle. Its three parts are connected and dependent upon one another. The first part of the adoption triangle is the birth parents. Sometimes birth parents make the difficult decision to place their child with another family. This scenario may occur when birth parents feel they are unable to give their child all the things they want them to have, such as two parents, or the basic essentials like food and clothes. In other cases, birth parents recognize they are too young and don't feel ready for the responsibilities of parenthood when faced with an unplanned pregnancy. Often, unselfish love and concern for their child leads birth parents to decide on an adoption.

Frequently, as happened in the case of my daughter, birth parents make a long "wish list" of specific things they want for their special child. The list for my daughter contained twenty items

"Our children need the benefits that a two-parent home can give. Birth parents can place their child for adoption and go on to live happy, fulfilled lives."[2]—Ruth A. Mark, ACSW, Executive Director, Adoption Resource Services

and included everything from "stay-at-home mom" to "a couple with a dog." My daughter's birth mother already knew her child would love dogs, and she was right! Birth parents may sort through literally hundreds of prospective couples before choosing just the right one for their child. They endure this painstaking process to make sure their child will be loved, happy, cherished, and part of a stable family.

The second part of the triangle is the adoptive family. Adoptive couples often face years of infertility and disappointments before they even begin the lengthy approval process to adopt. As couples take psychological tests, fill out seemingly endless forms, give social workers a tour of their homes, and endure personal interviews in order to complete their required home study, one thing keeps them going—the dream that one day they will have a child of their own to hold and love for the rest of their lives. This hope gives them the strength to persevere. Although adoptive couples usually have a long waiting period during which they have ample time to prepare and plan for

The author, Suzanne Slade, kissing her six-week-old adopted daughter, Christina.

The Long Wait for an International Adoption

Adoptive parents who want to adopt a child from another country often wait a long time before they finally bring home a child. The first step in an international adoption is to fill out the appropriate paperwork. Next is the referral, when the adoptive family is matched with a particular child. A referral will usually take between three and twelve months,[3] although in certain instances it can be shorter or longer. After that, parents endure an unknown waiting period before their child can come home. Most countries require adoptive parents to make at least one trip overseas, while some require several visits.

the arrival of their child, they are still nervous about becoming parents because they know parenting is a huge responsibility and they want to be the best parents in the whole world.

The final and completing part of the triangle is the adopted child—loved by birth parents and adoptive parents alike. Although this child is the center of much love, it's not uncommon for an adopted child, particularly in the teen years, to feel confused, upset, and at times not loved at all.

Am I for Real?

Some adopted teens experience times when they feel like they don't belong to normal or real family. Perhaps these feelings stem from the realization that th are not biologically connected to their parents and siblings. The cause of th doubts might also be a result of secrecy surrounding their past or birth famil teens question the authenticity of their family, they may also struggle with ings that their parents aren't their "real" parents. Some may even begin to if they aren't "real" themselves.

Teens Talk

Samantha, Age 18

"My mom loves to tell others what I used to say about my adoptio very young. I bet I've heard her repeat these words from my childh

When most people think of a family that is waiting to adopt a baby, they visualize a couple who struggles with infertility and is unable to have a child. This type of family is likely to be accepted by most adoption agencies and is often attractive to a birth mother when she reviews the available families at an agency. But there are many other kinds of families that hope to adopt a child as well.

A couple who already has a child, either by adoption or biologically, may be chosen by a birth family who wants their baby to have a sibling. But if a couple has had their own biological child, this may exclude them from being accepted by certain agencies that only work with infertile couples. Certain birth mothers are also less likely to choose a couple with a biological child because they fear their child would not be as special to the couple as the child or children already in the home.

Some people wishing to adopt, such as those who are single, or gay and lesbian couples, generally have a longer wait and face more obstacles than "traditional" couples, because some do not believe they fit the traditional definition of a family. Single women have been allowed to adopt children for years in the United tates, but it is very unusual for an unmarried, single man to break through the otypical ideals of who makes a suitable parent. Robert Klose, an unmarried professor, found out just how difficult it is for a single man to adopt. He d his quest to adopt a child in his book *Adopting Alyosha*. After three Robert finally found a child to call his own in a Russian orphanage.[4]

special cause I'm 'dopted.' Back then I couldn't say the word know what it meant either. All I knew was that my parents cial I was because I was adopted.

mewhere between then and now I've learned what the 'm not really sure *what* it means to be adopted. Oh, th mother loved me so much that she gave me to a by. My parents say they loved me when they first —before they even met me. I know my parents ll, most of the time). But somehow that story real. And I keep wondering—is this what a

"I feel like something's missing. Like there's this empty place inside me, almost like somebody died. And I think maybe my birth parents can fill that place or help me understand what that empty spot is. Or maybe I just

Webster's definition of *real*
—authentic, genuine[5]

need to know more about my birth parents. Perhaps I need to see that they're okay and hear for myself exactly why they placed me.

"All I know is—I want to belong to a real family. I want that empty place to go away, and I want to feel real."[6]

As a teen, life can seem very confusing as you move away from your childhood years and begin the lengthy process of becoming an adult. Sometimes you still feel like a kid. You want to just hang out with friends and goof around, instead of facing the more grown-up demands of school projects, term papers, and house chores. During those times you may hear parents or other adults tell you to act more responsibly and grown-up. Then there are other times when you feel more like an adult and you want to enjoy the privileges that adults have, like driving the car or staying out late. On the days you long to be treated like an adult, you may hear you aren't "old enough" or "mature enough" to do certain things. It's hard to feel like you are floating somewhere between being a child and an adult.

It can become overwhelming for adopted teens at times as they struggle with the normal changes that come with maturing and becoming an adult, along with having unresolved feelings about adoption. In the course of a single day, an adopted teen may feel special, happy, sad, anxious, mad, excited, confused, depressed, or many other feelings. Take comfort in knowing that all those feelings are okay and normal to have at times—whether you are adopted or not.

Is This for Real?

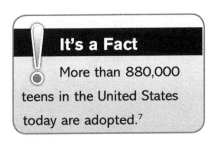

It's a Fact

More than 880,000 teens in the United States today are adopted.[7]

I've come to realize, from my daughter and other adopted children I know, that many adopted teens can carry a heavy burden of unanswered questions and pent-up feelings. I believe as teens open themselves up to examine their true emotions, needs, and questions, they will experience a more positive and healthy adoption journey. This book was written to serve as a guide to help adopted teens explore their feelings, face their uncertainties, and find answers to the questions they must ask. Along the way they may also decide, as many have, that adoption can create genuine, supportive, helpful, generous, crazy, loving, and really *real* families.

My daughter, Christina, as a teen with her birth mother, Christy. Shortly after Christina turned nine, her adoption was opened at her request (after receiving approval from the social worker at the agency that placed her). Christina enjoys a warm and affirming relationship with her birth mother. This photo was taken at Christy's home during their week-long visit in July 2006.

Notes

1. Christine Adamec and William L. Pierce, *The Encyclopedia of Adoption* (New York: Facts on File, Inc., 2000), xv.
2. Ruth Mark, telephone interview, August 14, 2006.
3. "How Long Does Adoption Take?" *Adoptive Families* (June 2006), 12.
4. Robert Klose, *Adopting Alyosha* (Jackson: University Press of Mississippi, 1999).
5. *Webster's New Universal Unabridged Dictionary* (New York: Simon & Schuster, 1972), 1501.
6. Samantha (name changed), author interview, May 25, 2006.
7. Child Welfare Information Gateway, "How Many Children Were Adopted in 2000 and 2001? Numbers and Trends," 2004, www.childwelfare.gov/pubs/s_adopted/s_adoptedf.cfm (accessed March 29, 2012). [Note: In 1992, 2000, and 2001, an average of 127,000 adoptions was recorded. That average, multiplied by seven years, results in about 889,000 adopted teens living in the United States in 2012.]

Reader's Note

After *Adopted: The Ultimate Teen Guide* was published, I received requests from several adoption groups for discussion questions. I compiled a list of those questions, which I have included at the end of each chapter in this new edition. Readers may decide to study this book from front to back or choose to peruse chapters most relevant to them. For example, teens interested in issues about birth parents might focus on chapters 4 ("Why Did My Birth Parents Choose Adoption?"), 5 ("Should I Search?"), 6 ("Searching for Birth Parents"), and 7 ("Meeting Birth Parents"). A group of internationally adopted teens might benefit most from chapters 2 ("Fitting In"), 8 ("International Adoptions"), 9 ("Transracial Adoption"), and 10 ("A Real Family").

Please remember, there are no right or wrong answers to these discussion questions. A successful group is one that provides a safe place where teens can acknowledge and verbalize their thoughts, questions, fears, and unresolved feelings about adoption—where they can hear others' stories and find support and encouragement as they search for answers to their questions.

FINDING OUT YOU'RE ADOPTED

*"There has always been this sign hanging in my room for as long as I can remember—
'You were not grown under my heart, but in it.' That's how I knew I was adopted.
It's no big deal. Being adopted is OK."[1]—Billy, age 19*

*"I always knew I was adopted, probably because I can't remember back far enough
to a point where I did not know. I thought everyone was adopted, because both
my brother and I were. I thought it was normal."[2]—Alanna, age 18*

Many adopted children grow up hearing they are "adopted," but most do not fully comprehend what that means until adolescence, when they gain a better understanding of the legal system and "the facts of life." Other adopted children are not told they are adopted until they reach a certain age. No matter when you learn about your adoption, it may be hard to imagine having any other parents than the ones you've grown up calling "Mom" and "Dad." You may also find you have a bunch of unanswered questions. *Why didn't my birth mother want me? Was there something wrong with me? Where are my birth parents? Do I look like them?*

Discovering You Look Different

Children perceive physical differences between themselves and their adoptive parents at a very young age, usually by preschool. The inheritance of detailed characteristics, such as eye shape or hair color, is a sophisticated concept that may not be understood by a child until he or she studies biology later in school. While children adopted by parents of the same race notice differences between themselves and their adoptive parents, they may not connect those differences to the fact that they are adopted until their teen years.

"Finding out you're adopted"

(c) C Papile 1997

However, as early as three or four years of age, children know that they belong to a racial group that is distinguished from other groups by certain physical differences. Transracially adopted children usually connect the differences in appearance between themselves and their adoptive parents to their adoption at a rather early age, before they fully understand what adoption means.

Whenever this defining moment occurs for an adopted child, whether in a same-race or transracial adoptive family, the realization that his or her appearance does not resemble either parent may cause confusion and fear. This child may even feel like he or she doesn't belong in his or her family. Recognizing differences in appearance can lead adopted children to investigate and gain a greater realization of what adoption means. Often, the teenage years are when a child begins to fully understand adoption and asks the question, "Who am I?"

The Grieving Process

When you suddenly discover, or more fully understand the fact that you are adopted, it's not uncommon to go through a grieving process that is very similar to the grief experienced after someone dies. You may feel like you have "lost" your birth parents, although you have never really known them. And if you feel that way, it may be difficult to find an outlet for your sadness because most of the people around you won't experience this type of grief and therefore don't understand it. Perhaps you even feel guilty about experiencing this sense of loss

Dr. Christopher Papile supplied the adoption cartoon on page 2, and three others in this book. He is the founder of www.Adopted Life.com, a popular website that features his adoption cartoons, paintings, and other valuable resources such as poetry, e-postcards, and a posting page where searching birth parents and adoptees can place their contact information. His cartoons have appeared on many websites and in print. Through AdoptedLife, Dr. Papile has helped numerous organizations, such as the Alabama Foster Parent Association (representing over 3,000 foster family homes) and FAIR, a Palo Alto, California-based organization offering support to adoptive and preadoptive families.

Dr. Papile has a bachelor's and PhD in chemical engineering and works extensively in the alternative energy field. He also studied painting at the Pennsylvania Academy of the Fine Arts and enjoys using his creativity to benefit the environment and humanity.

because you have a great adoptive family. It may help to know that feelings of grief are common for adopted children when they become old enough to fully comprehend what "being adopted" means.[3] If you experience feelings of grief and loss due to your adoption, it's important to permit yourself to acknowledge and express those emotions.

Today most adopted children grow up knowing they are adopted. Adoption isn't a big secret like it was years ago. But that doesn't necessarily make it easier

It's a Fact

Adoption practices vary greatly from country to country and from generation to generation. For example, as recently as in the 1970s, U.S. adoptions were secretive, and adoptive couples often went to great lengths in order to keep others from finding out their child was adopted. To make sure their adoption went undetected, couples typically adopted only babies of their own race.

Recently, adoption practices have changed dramatically. Today families commonly adopt children of other races, infants from other countries, children with special needs, and older children. Current adoption practices tend to emphasize the needs of the adopted child over the wishes of the adoptive family.[4]

It's a Fact

Every year many adoptive families celebrate the day their adoptive child came home in their own special way on "Gotcha Day." This phrase refers to the day the adoptive family "got" their child. Some adopted children choose their favorite restaurant for a family dinner out on their Gotcha Day, while others may receive gifts. Families have different ways they like to celebrate this special day, while some may not choose to recognize it at all. One adoptive parent, Margaret Schwartz, decided to name September 15 as the first International Gotcha Day in 2005.[5]

to understand. Even if you have been told since you were a baby that you're adopted, you still may experience a time when your adoption "hits you in the face." When you become old enough to more fully understand what adoption means, the whole thing can suddenly feel overwhelming. As a teen, you may be discovering new feelings about your birth family that you haven't felt before. You may have questions about your adoption that you never thought of when you were younger. It's very common for adopted teens to rethink their adoption and what it means to them.

Faith and her adoptive mother, Donna

My Story–Faith, Age 18

When I was 14 I started to think a lot about my birth mother. One week I was really struggling with school and friends and figuring out who I was. It seemed everything was hitting me all at the same time. That week I got overwhelmed and felt insecure about myself and where I came from. I ended up crying so hard one night I couldn't seem to stop. I asked my mom why I didn't have any pictures or anything from my birth mother. I knew my brother, who was also adopted, had a lot of pictures and stuff from his birth mother. Finally my mother told me she did have a letter and a picture of my birth parents. She said they were in a safety deposit box and we could get them in the morning. She also explained that my birth mother was my age, 14, when she had me. Then I began to understand why she couldn't keep me. That was the longest night of my life. I am so grateful that my birth mother had me, and gave me a family who loves me so much. Her gift to me is priceless.

Ever since that night I always think about my birth mother on my birthday. And I know that even though she doesn't know me, we have a connection because we shared one special day together—the day I was born.[6]

Take Your Time

Knowing that most adopted teens face a very confusing time like this can help you not "freak out" when it happens. Remember, you don't have to understand and figure out everything in one day. Your parents love you and will answer your questions and help you sort out your feelings. You might also have a friend who is adopted that you could talk to. And there are adoption groups that meet all over the country to help kids work through their different emotions. The feelings you are having are normal. So give yourself time to learn about and understand your adoption.

Finding Out When You're Older

If you find out you are adopted when you are older, it can be a huge shock. It may seem like everything you thought was true isn't. You may feel like the people

Mary, a birth mother who placed her daughter with an adoptive family when she was first born, uses art as a way to release her feelings of love for her daughter and the longing she had to see her again. This drawing depicts the love between a mother and child.

you love and trust the most have lied to you. If you find yourself in this situation, tell your parents how you feel. Give them the opportunity to explain why they decided to tell you when you were older. Maybe they have some very good reasons for waiting, and maybe they don't. But remember, your parents probably chose the timing and way they wanted to share this information based on what they thought would be best for you. Take your time and work through your feelings. Maybe you could join a group of other kids who recently learned they were adopted. A support group is a great place to talk about your feelings and to be

> ### ❗ It's a Fact
>
> The ancient Roman civilization allowed adoptions and even had adoption laws. The well-known Roman ruler Julius Caesar adopted his nephew Octavian. In fact, Julius Caesar's dynasty was carried on through Octavian when he became Caesar Augustus.[7]

heard and understood. Hearing others' stories may give you some answers that you've been looking for, and you might share something that really helps someone else. In the back of this book you will find a list of some websites that will help you find a group in your area.

Reva's Story

Reva was shocked when she found out her parents had been keeping a secret from her for her entire life. She was in her early thirties when she learned she was adopted. Reva shares the details of her discovery:

> Growing up as an only child, I felt that somehow I didn't belong in my family—a feeling that seemed out of place in my small, Midwest hometown. Something wasn't quite right and I couldn't put my finger on what it was, but it persisted throughout my childhood. I remember especially as a teenager struggling with these feelings and wondering what was wrong with me that I felt this way.
>
> After my father died, I discovered a short note dated three months after I was born that provided a clue to those early feelings of discontent. This handwritten note stated, "She [Reva] deserves you and you her. I know I'll never regret what I've done." I did not recognize the name of the woman who signed the letter. *Who was she? What did this mean? Was I adopted?* I shared the note with people I trusted to gather their opinions, and they all agreed—someone had given up a baby for adoption. But I just couldn't bring myself to believe this could be true. *If it were true, that meant that my parents had been lying to me my whole life.* And if they lied about something this big, what else had been a lie? Was "I love you" a lie?
>
> I wanted facts to prove or disprove my suspicions, and asked a neighbor who was an attorney to search the county records to see if there was any information about my parents adopting a baby. He didn't find any adoption records in their name, so I decided to put these crazy ideas to rest. I remember thinking this might be something I just wasn't supposed

to know. I told God, "If I am supposed to know anything more about this, you'll have to give me skywriting. I'll ask no more questions."

I pushed the thoughts of adoption out of my mind and went on with my busy life. I was living in Colorado and enjoying my career in nursing. God had given me a wonderful church family and I was content. Just two weeks after putting this to rest, I browsed through the church directory looking for a friend's phone number and something caught my eye. I saw "Reva" but it wasn't me; there was a different last name. It was the same name of the woman I had been named after back in Indiana! Could this be her—thirty years later and 2,000 miles away? I had not had any contact with her since I was ten years old.

We made arrangements to meet and what a sweet reunion it was. She was now almost 80 years old and living in a nursing home. I waited anxiously during our visit for the right time to ask her about the mystery of my birth. It didn't take but a few minutes. She made reference to, "Before your folks got you . . ." *What? Got me?* My heart pounded in my chest, as I knew I was on the edge of the truth. My palms were moist and my throat dry as I asked the big question, *"Are you telling me I was adopted?"* She replied, "Oh, my! They never told you? Did I let the cat out of the bag?"

It was the most bittersweet moment of my life. The revealed truth relieved the lifelong burden of wondering. And at the same time it meant that I had been lied to. What happened? My adoptive mother confessed they had withheld this information from me, thinking it was the right thing to do. But she had the name of my birth mother, so I continued to investigate and tried to track down the location of this mystery woman. Now things were moving at a dizzying speed and a friend located her by searching on the Internet. I was afraid to call her myself for fear she would deny it or not want anything to do with me. The thought of being given away twice was too much for me.

My pastor called her, and indeed I was her child and my parents had adopted me. My first conversation with her on the phone was filled with tears and laughter. She wanted to see me as much as I wanted to see her. When we met it was strange to sit across the table from this woman—my mother, and see myself in the shape of her nose and identical hands. It was a wonderful surprise to learn that I had brothers and sisters after having been an only child my whole life. My birth family welcomed me in as if I had always been there. I feel blessed, as I know many who have been adopted never get this luxury. My birth family has not replaced the family I had prior to meeting them but has filled in the missing pieces of the puzzle.

In the years since my discovery of my adoption, I have had to work through some mixed emotions about my adoptive parents' decision to keep my adoption secret. I later learned my father had burned all of my adoption paperwork in order to keep me from finding out. I also struggled with forgiving my birth mother for giving me away. It is only my relationship with God and the mercy of the Lord that has helped me with this. God forgave me for my sins by sending his son Jesus Christ to die on the cross. It is by his example and grace that I can forgive.

What I learned when I got to know my birth mother was that giving me up for adoption was the most difficult and courageous thing she ever did. Giving me up was an act of love I can hardly take in. In Psalms 139 God tells me this: "For you created my inmost being; you knit me together in my mother's womb! I praise you because I am fearfully and wonderfully made; your works are wonderful; I know that full well . . . all the days ordained for me were written in your book before one of them came to be" (NIV). He knew me before I was born and that the perfect plan for my life was to be born to a woman who would not raise me. While I may question many things over my lifetime, there is no question of how much God loves me and orchestrated my life starting with my birth and adoption.[8]

One Rapper's Adoption Journey

When Darryl McDaniels, known as "DMC" of the rap group RUN-DMC, was thirty-five he started to write his autobiography. During that writing process, Darryl's whole world changed when his mother, Banna McDaniels, shared that she and her husband, Byford, had adopted him when he was three months old. Darryl was surprised to discover he was born to a teenage girl in Queens, New York, on May 31, 1964. Darryl decided he wanted to meet his birth mother and

"Life is not perfect and people make mistakes; life has difficulties to be solved. Birth parents place their child because they love and care for that child more than they care about themselves. They had a situation that was difficult and they solved it in the best way they could at the time. It helps to have a grateful attitude rather than a critical one. It also helps to try to understand their situation and to put yourself in their shoes."[9]
—Ruth A. Mark, ACSW, Executive Director, Adoption Resource Services

that he also wanted to make his search public. In 2006, his adoption story and search for his birth mother was aired on VH1 as a reality show, *DMC: My Adoption Journey.*

Despite the fact that Darryl's adoption was closed, he was eventually able to find and meet his birth mother. He also discovered he has a sister and two brothers. Darryl hopes to find his biological father in the future. Because of the difficulties Darryl experienced trying to obtain his original birth certificate, he is trying to help change current laws so that all adoption records will be opened for searching adoptees.

Darryl wrote a song titled "Just Like Me" to honor everyone in the adoption triangle. He hopes this song helps end some of the shame and guilt surrounding adoption. He wants people to focus on what adoption is really about—love.

From his own reunion experiences, Darryl advises adoptees to take it slow when meeting members of their birth family. He shares that even though these people may be biologically related to you, you can't expect an immediate and close bond. DMC believes a reunion of birth family members goes best if people don't have enormous expectations.[10]

Teens Talk

Sasha, Age 19

No one, specifically, ever had to break the news to me that I was adopted. I guess for a lot of kids it may not be as "visually" apparent, the wounds may be more embedded, but to be a brown child in a white family is never invisible. For every stare my family gets when we go out, every 'is this/are you together?' in a checkout line, every presumptive question that someone puts in my face; I say, these are the people that told me I was adopted. In their prejudice, in their ignorance, in their questions; it didn't need to be spoken. It was enforced everywhere we went.[11]

Laura, Age 18

From the time that I can remember I have known I was adopted. As a child, I really wasn't aware of what it meant. As I grew up I began to realize just what my life was all about. My parents never discussed the fact that my sister and I were adopted, so we assumed it was not a subject to converse about.

Even so, not a day passes that I don't think about my unique situation. Sometimes, I find myself asking these questions over and over: Who are my natural par-

When some children learn they are adopted, the news comes as a real surprise, but for some adoptees, more surprises still lie ahead. This was the case for a girl who once lived in an orphanage in Yangzhou, China. She was later adopted by a family, Holly and Douglas Funk and their five biological children, from Lyons, Illinois. Before leaving for China to pick up their newest family member in July 2004, the Funks named their daughter Mia. More than a year later, in October of 2005, another family made the long trip to the Yangzhou Children's Welfare Institute in China. The Ramirez family, Carlos and Diana and their two sons, arrived in China and adopted a little girl named Mia Hanying. Mia was twenty-eight months old when she flew to the United States with her new family to their home in Miami, Florida.

The Funk and Ramirez families had no connection with one another until they met via the Internet in May 2006. Diana Ramirez had posted an entry about Mia's upcoming birthday on a website for families that had adopted children from the Yangzhou Children's Welfare Institute. Holly Funk noticed the posting. She e-mailed back that she also had a daughter the same age with the same birthday. The two mothers then compared pictures of the girls and other background information and began to wonder if they were twins. The girls' parents decided to use DNA testing to find out. A swab from Mia Funk's and Mia Ramirez's mouths confirmed what their parents had suspected—the girls are very likely twins. The official lab results indicate an 85 percent probability that at a minimum, the girls are half-sisters. The only way to know with 100 percent certainty is to have a biological parent complete DNA testing, which would be very difficult since the adoptive families do not have access to the birth parents' names. But with all the facts the families do have, they feel rather confident the girls are fraternal twins.

Although the girls had talked to each other over the phone, they were reunited for the first time in August 2006 in Chicago. The two were shy at first, but soon warmed up to each other and held hands. It seemed to be the beginning of a lifelong friendship, as the parents of both girls hope to visit each other often.

Increasingly, more and more adopted teens are using modern technology, such as the Internet and DNA testing, to unlock secrets that have been hidden for years. Internet sites dedicated to helping adoptees find their birth parents provide a place for both parties to post their personal information. Sometimes these postings lead to reunions. DNA testing has become popular in recent years and is useful to help identify biological bonds. It is also used to provide some information on the racial background of an adopted person when no other records exist.[12]

"Adoption is an intense, deep, emotional experience because it involves love and concern for the entire future of a precious human being."[9]—Ruth A. Mark, ACSW, executive director of Adoption Resource Services

ents? Are they alive? Does my mother ever think about me? What does she look like? Does she live around here? Have I passed her on the street? Sometimes I think that wondering about my other set of parents means I'm being ungrateful to the parents who have loved and cared for me for the past eighteen years. Although I just can't help but wonder about these things, I do think it's natural for adoptees to feel the need to talk about their natural parents. I just thank God every day that my natural mother made the decision to put me up for adoption and gave me a chance to live instead of so selfishly taking my life through abortion.[13]

Liana, Age 17

Ever since I can remember, I always knew I was adopted. My parents always believed in letting me know right away; thinking that it was wrong to keep that big of a "secret" from a child. I remember reading books on adoption, my brother (who is also adopted) and I would always read the same book over and over. One of our favorite books was *A Mother for Choco* by Keiko Kasza. This book really explained what adoption is and how this unusual bird is looking for a mom and eventually ends up having a bear as a mom.

When my mother and father told me I was adopted, it never really sank in until I was older. People would ask, "Why do you look different from your parents?" and I would say, "I was adopted." My parents also found an "adoptive group" where a group of families would get together and socialize every so often. It was our own little group and we would see each other for years. This enabled

A Mother for Choco is a picture book written and illustrated by Keiko Kasza. This classic tale highlights the fact that everyone is special and unique, and teaches the importance of acceptance and love. It has been translated into French, Polish, Korean, Chinese, Hebrew, and Spanish. Adopted children in many parts of the world enjoy reading about Choco, the little bird that goes searching for a mother that looks like him and ends up finding a loving family comprised of many different kinds of animals. The book was first published in Japan. It was later published in the United States in 1992 by Putnam after the text was changed to English. The original color pencil drawings were also redone by Ms. Kasza using gouache, a media similar to watercolor.

Interestingly, the author did not have adoption in mind when she wrote the story. Keiko Kasza was born and raised in Japan, and the story was based on her observations when she first arrived in the United States. Ms. Kasza shares what happened that day:

I was twenty-one when I first came to the United States. I landed in Los Angeles and was surprised to see people of so many races walking around in the airport. You can imagine my shock coming from such a homogeneous country, Japan. There are a few experiences in people's lives that are engraved forever. That was one of those moments for me. I never thought about adoption when I wrote the story. The reaction from the adoption community has been wonderful. It was a huge surprise to me—a nice surprise! I have been invited to talk to adoption groups. The people I meet in those situations always impress me. They are such caring parents.[14]

my brother and me to realize that we weren't the only ones adopted and it's not unusual. Basically, I always knew I was adopted but never fully understood what it meant until our adoptive group would get together. It made me feel special, almost unique. I mean, why do people try to be so much alike, when we were born to be different? When I fully understood what it meant and actually let it sink in, it didn't bother me at all. I'm thankful for what I have; although, questions still come up to the surface about my birth mother.[15]

Michael, Age 17

I remember being told I was adopted when I was about four or five. I sometimes would notice that everyone around me was different than I was, but I told myself that it was normal. As I got to the age of seven I was very aware and I wasn't quite sure that I would fit in my community. Now I'm seventeen and no matter what, I don't care what people think because I know I am unique and whatever my life has to do with someone else is fine by me.[16]

When Friends Find Out

Although you may have worked through many of your feelings after discovering you were adopted, you will probably also have to learn how to respond to others when they first find out. Many people have heard false information or prejudiced statements, or have developed their own misconceptions about adoption. One of the most obvious and annoying ways this misinformation affects adoptees is in the form of insensitive questions.

Arm Yourself

Difficult questions usually lead to an uncomfortable exchange for both you and the person asking the question. You can avoid being thrown off guard or embarrassed if you prepare yourself for certain commonly asked questions. Here are a few that you've probably already heard:

- "Do you know where your real mother is?"
- "Why didn't your parents keep you?"
- "Where are you from?"
- "Can you speak Korean?" (for teens born in another country [e.g., Korea])

If you seem to hear the same questions over and over, take some time to form the answers that work well for you. Armed with a ready response, you won't be taken by surprise.

Suppose a friend asks, "Do you know where your real mother is?" Possible answers you might give:

- "Do you mean my birth mother? She lives in Iowa." *or*
- "My mother is at home (or work)."

"Why didn't your parents keep you?"

- "My birth parents made an adoption plan for me because they weren't ready to be parents yet." *or*
- "I don't usually share that information."

"Where are you from?"

- "I grew up on the south side of town, but now I live on Maple Avenue." *or*
- "I'm not sure what you mean. Are you asking that because I'm adopted?" *or*
- "I was born in Texas, and an agency there placed me with my parents."

"Can you speak Korean?"

- "I grew up in the United States just like you, so I only know English." *or*
- "I left Korea when I was two weeks old. I have a great memory, but not that good!"

Nontraditional Family

Some people in our society still define a family as a married couple with biological children. These people have not broadened their view and realized that there are various nontraditional family models. Healthy, loving, and very real families are created in many ways. A large number of families today are single-parent, have a grandparent acting in the parenting role, or are formed when two families blend together due to divorce and remarriage. Others may have one grandparent and one parent working together as the heads of the household, while some have two parents of the same sex. Adoption also creates families that are very real but don't happen to fall within the traditional definition of a family. Unfortunately, the burden of teaching others about nontraditional families often falls on those who belong to those types of families.

What about You?

As a teen, you probably have a greater understanding of what adoption means than when you were young. This broader knowledge may have created some new questions and unsettled emotions. You may not know exactly what will help you work through your complicated feelings about being adopted, or how to find answers to your questions at this point in your life.

Educating Others

One way you can be proactive and head off potentially inappropriate questions about adoption is to make a presentation to certain groups, such as a sports team or an organization you belong to, or at school. Your teacher may welcome the opportunity to enrich the class and learn more about the topic of adoption. Classes such as social studies or life skills may be the perfect place to share your story. If you find the idea of standing in front of a group terrifying, your teacher might be willing to let your parent talk to the class or bring information for the teacher to present to the class about what it's like to be adopted.

Here are a few key points you can share with other teens and teachers to help them understand more about adoption.

1. Families formed by adoption are "real" families — Your adoptive parents are just like other parents. They love, teach, discipline, and care for you just like biological parents.
2. Adoption is a safe topic — By openly discussing the adoption, you help others realize that adoption is a natural part of your life and you aren't embarrassed to talk about it. They will learn that it is a significant part of who you are and that they don't need to be afraid to bring it up.
3. Placing a child is a difficult, unselfish, and loving choice — Share that a birth mother who places her child is not "giving up," but rather intentionally making a plan for her child and for the type of life she wants that child to have. Most birth parents invest a great deal of time and effort when selecting the adoptive family for their child. They select a particular family based on factors that they feel are important, such as a stay-at-home mom, a couple that has been married for several years, or a certain religious background. Some birth parents may also consider if the family has other siblings or even pets.

One simple place to start is a heart-to-heart discussion with one or both of your parents. They might be able to give you many of the answers you need. This chapter explained that some adopted children experience a sense of loss and very real grief when they gain a more mature understanding of adoption. If you experience these types of feelings, allow yourself to grieve. Talk about these emotions with a parent or a trusted friend. Perhaps joining an adoption support group would provide you with an outlet to share your feelings. Educating those around you on the topic of adoption might also help you feel more in control of your life and your adoption situation.

As you continue to learn more about adoption, hopefully you will discover information that is useful and pertinent to your unique adoption situation. And that's what this book is all about—sharing other adopted teens' thoughts and experiences and providing resources, new ideas, and advice from adoption professionals that will help equip you for your personal adoption journey ahead.

Discussion Questions

When and how did you find out you were adopted?

Do you remember how you felt when you first found out?

How do you feel today about being adopted?

Do people ever ask you questions about your adoption?

What's the best way you've found to handle nosy or annoying questions?

Notes

1. Billy, author interview, April 6, 2005.
2. Alanna, e-mail correspondence, March 10, 2006.
3. *Factsheet: Impact of Adoption on Adopted Persons* (Washington, DC: National Adoption Information Clearinghouse, 2004).
4. Barbara Moe, *Adoption* (Santa Barbara, CA: ABC-CLIO, 1998), 1.
5. Karen Moline, "Get Rid of 'GOTCHA,'" *Adoptive Families* (January/February 2006), 29.
6. Faith, author interview, April 17, 2006.
7. Christine Adamec and William L. Pierce, *The Encyclopedia of Adoption* (New York: Facts on File, Inc., 2000), xv.
8. Reva, telephone interview, December 19, 2006.
9. Ruth Mark, telephone interview, August 14, 2006.
10. *Interview with DMC: More about "My Adoption Journey,"* at adoption.about.com/od/adoptionissues/a/dmcinterview.htm (accessed July 24, 2006).

11. Sasha, e-mail correspondence, March 4, 2006.

12. Russell Working, "Separated at Birth, United by Chance," *Chicago Tribune*, August 20, 2006, 1.

13. Laura (name changed), author interview, September 6, 2006.

14. Keiko Kasza, e-mail correspondence, September 3 and 5, 2006.

15. Liana, e-mail correspondence, March 22, 2006.

16. Michael, e-mail correspondence, March 29, 2006.

2

FITTING IN

*"I feel different from my family all the time. Being adopted, I realize I will
probably never have heart disease like my father or bad arthritis like my mother.
I realize that I am also a lot more easygoing than my parents. I feel like this is my home;
however, I feel different in my home. It's hard to describe, but I feel loved and at the
same time different and separated."[1]—Michael, age 17*

Do you remember the last time you put a puzzle together? Did you find a piece
that looked like it was the perfect size, shape, and color to fit in a certain spot,
but then when you tried to place it in the puzzle, it didn't fit at all? As a teen, you
may feel like a puzzle piece that doesn't quite fit sometimes. Perhaps you feel like
you don't fit at school, at home, or both.

No doubt about it, the teen years can be rough. Everything is changing so
fast—your body, your emotions, and your feelings. Your body is also beginning
to produce hormones, and the strong feelings that can accompany them are new
and sometimes difficult to understand. Your face may be under constant attack by
acne, you might have grown several inches taller in the last year, and clothes that
are the perfect size one week may not come close to fitting the next.

But often, the hardest part of being a teen is feeling like you don't fit in. Teenagers tend to hang out together in small groups, or cliques, and the list of who's
"in" and who's "out" can change almost daily. And if trying to fit in at school isn't
hard enough, sometimes it's even harder to feel like you fit in at home. Parents
may have rules and expectations that seem impossible to meet. Annoying brothers
and sisters can be a pain to live with and add to your difficulties at home.

Knowing Who You Are

One of the keys to fitting in with your adoptive family lies in understanding and
knowing who you are. Realizing your own identity helps you feel secure around
others. So what is an identity and how do you find yours? Contrary to many of

the television and magazine ads that target teens, your identity is not based solely on your appearance. The fact that you may or may not look like other members of your family has no bearing on who you are. Your identity is much more than just DNA or genes. Many factors throughout your developing years, such as your interests, relationships, race, culture, experiences, studies, travel, have slowly shaped who you have become, your identity. Teens in search of their identity need to reflect on their past and how they have been changed through their experiences. Recognizing your true interests and the things you are passionate about, instead of following the crowd, can also provide clues to your identity. Examining your values, the close relationships in your life, and the many roles you have will help you further assess who you truly are.

For the adopted teen the question of "Who am I?" often requires more time and information to answer than for other teens. Adopted teens need to not only define themselves in terms of self, family, and friends, but they also need to explore and incorporate their adoption into that definition. Realizing that they are biologically connected to two people who made the decision to place them with another family may seem like a simple thought, but many adopted teens ignore or are unable to process the emotions they feel as they consider this fact.

Teens Talk

Billy, Age 19

Billy, age nineteen, shares his views on the things in his life that have helped shape his identity:

> Being adopted isn't a big deal to me. The only connection I have with my birth mother and father is genes. I have always held the view that genes really aren't a big deal, it's not who you are. I put much more weight on nurture rather than nature.
>
> I think that almost all aspects of our personality can be traced back to how we were raised. I am who I am due to the experiences that I have had, my reaction (whether positive or negative) to my parents, geographic location, time period, and economic situation. There are a lot of factors, but in no way do I feel connected with my birth mother. I look up to her for not having an abortion, which I wouldn't have blamed her if she had. She was a young girl carrying a baby she wasn't going to keep, that's something really honorable. I feel I have a connection to the obvious character she had. I guess it's like a stranger you've heard about and just think they are pretty badass. I feel that biological moms, dads, and all that are nothing to hold onto, or hold as what an adopted kid is.

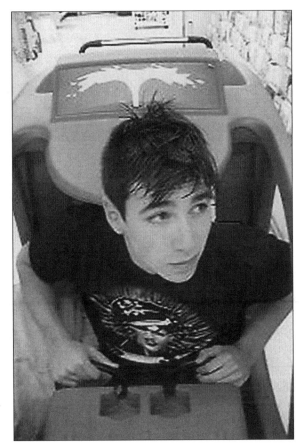

Billy on a roller coaster

Too many adopted kids put their problems, lack of self-identity, and general feelings of distance with their families on the fact that they were adopted. I can't speak for those adopted in their later years, but as for those adopted before they can remember or even before five, they need to let go. It's just a chemical reaction. You're where you are for a reason. And if not even that, it's where you are, and you owe that to what you've been surrounded by. I am guessing I am nothing like my birth parents besides physically looking alike, and there is no sense in feeling a connection on solely that.[2]

Self-Esteem

Another factor to consider when you feel like you don't fit in is self-esteem. Simply put, self-esteem is how you feel about yourself or the amount of value you believe you have to those around you. Some adopted teens feel unwanted because their birth parents placed them in another home. This perceived rejection can lead to feelings of low self-worth and insignificance. If you struggle with these types of feelings and haven't had the opportunity to talk about the reasons behind your adoption with one of your birth parents, then it may be helpful for you to do some research. One place to start is to simply ask your parents what information they have regarding your birth parents' decision to place you. You can also check out chapter 4. Personal stories of several birth mothers and their reasons for placing their children, along with the overriding feelings of love they express for their babies, are included in that chapter. Reading others' stories, and perhaps discovering the reasons your birth mother chose to place you, may provide some answers that will help boost your self-esteem. Once you gain an understanding of your birth mother's situation and her hopes for your life, you may come to a place where you can trade in your feelings of rejection for appreciation of her unselfish love and concern for you.

Getting Along with Parents

All children want to feel loved and connected to their mom and dad, or the main caregiver of the family. If you don't feel understood or compatible with your parents much of the time, as an adopted teen it can be tempting to blame genetics, loss of bonding time in the womb, or other reasons that have to do with your adoption. While very real differences may exist between you and your parents due to the fact you are not related biologically (such as temperament, interests, physical appearance, and even seemingly small things like sleeping or eating habits), you can't assume that all of your relational issues hinge on adoption-related problems.

If you want to strengthen your family relationships, then resist spending all your time and energy battling over the small stuff, like your hairstyle, clothes, music, or the pile of steamed broccoli at dinner. Instead, try focusing your energy on the big stuff, such as building trust, respect, truth, communication, and unconditional love. By spending your time on what is most important in your relationship with your parents, you can build some bridges and feel closer to them.

Another thing to remember is that your parents aren't mind readers. If your family is one that encourages everyone to talk openly, take the time to share that you sometimes feel like an outsider and give them the opportunity to express their feelings and reassure you that you do belong. If your family tends to talk about things on the surface but is usually hesitant to discuss deeper emotions, you may need to break some new ground by revealing your true feelings. The very idea of a heart-to-heart discussion with your parents may seem scary, but try pushing through your fears. The payoff is worth it. By sharing your true thoughts and emotions, your parents will become more sensitive to your needs and feelings. Remember, they love you more than you know, and most likely they would like to be closer to you, too.

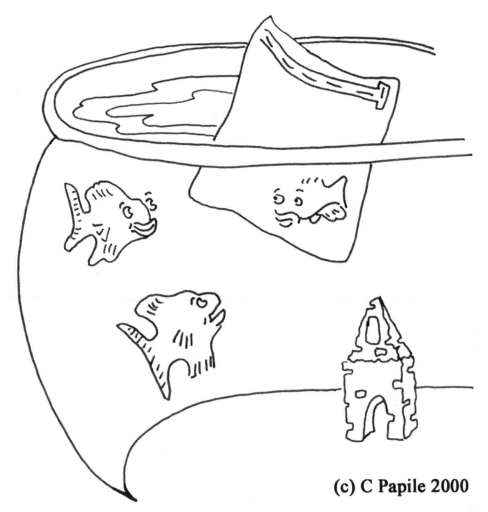

(c) C Papile 2000

Warming up to adoptive parents

If this approach doesn't work, or you can't move past your fears to give it a try, you could find someone else you trust. Perhaps you could confide in a close friend, school counselor, or a family friend from your place of worship. This person might be able to help you explain your thoughts to your family later. If you can find a way to honestly communicate with your parents, this will most likely result in a closer relationship with them.

Getting Along with Siblings

Have you ever felt like you have absolutely nothing in common with your brothers or sisters? Do your siblings seem to delight in annoying you, and know just the right button to push to make you angry? Does it seem like their sole purpose is to make your life miserable?

As an adopted teen, you might want to jump to the conclusion that the reason you don't get along with your siblings is because you do not share a biological connection with them. You may believe that because there are so many genetic differences between you, getting along is impossible. You might even hold the belief that if you were truly related to your brothers and sisters, you would not only share a more similar outward appearance, but you would also have an easy, congenial relationship because you share the same likes, dislikes, interests, etc.

Well, guess what—you're not the first adopted teen to come up with this idea. In fact, it is a rather common thought among adoptees. But if you observe families in which all the siblings are blood related, you'll soon discover this theory doesn't hold up very well. You might notice that biological siblings disagree and fight, just as adopted siblings do. The same trend is true with the positive interactions in families. Brought together by adoption or birth, siblings in all families also have times where they encourage and support one another.

Experts have found that sibling relationships form as children grow up and share similar experiences and events. The good times you spend with your family, such as a ski trip, a day at an amusement park, or a family celebration, and also the hard things, like a death in the family, sharing a room, or even sharing the phone, are the events that over time form the special relationships you have with your siblings. The fact that you and your brothers or sisters have been raised in a similar way, by the same set of parents, creates a complex and unique bond. "Doing life together," not DNA, creates a lifelong link and the special relationships between brothers and sisters. And siblings will have their ups and downs. They will not always agree or even like each other.

So how do you develop better relationships with your brothers or sisters, or feel like you fit in? What can you do to have more positive than negative interactions? One way is to simply try to notice the good qualities in your siblings, or the ways they are helpful, rather than only focusing on their annoying habits. Say "thanks" when they give you a ride or share their new CD. They will appreciate the kind words and might even shoot a few back your way. You could also try to think of all the things you have in common. You may discover that there are many activities or sports you both enjoy. If you share a love of baseball with your brother, ask him to a ball game. Attend a concert with your sister. These may seem like simple things to do, but sometimes going to a fun event that you both enjoy can help you realize just how great your siblings can be. Spend time with your parents and siblings. Enjoy them for who they are—your family.

We're Okay

Although fitting in with family and friends and at school is generally an issue for teens, adoption doesn't necessarily make fitting in more difficult. "I don't experience feelings of not fitting in because I'm adopted" was a common response given by many teens interviewed for this book. In particular, teens who belong to the same race as their parents and were adopted as infants and raised with other adopted siblings seemed to believe that adoption had not affected how they fit in at home or socially. And many children adopted into transracial families and those adopted at an older age also reported that they just seemed to naturally fit in with their adoptive families.

Teens Talk

Alanna, Age 18

Alanna, age eighteen, is an African American teen who was adopted by a Caucasian family. She does not focus on the differing shades of skin in her home but instead emphasizes the love and many opportunities her adoptive family has given her. She tries to appreciate the special family members in her life:

Alanna

> I feel grateful. I feel *extremely* lucky. I could have ended up with any family, but I got an amazing one. I have had so many opportunities because of it. I lived in England for five years of my life and traveled in Europe and Africa. I have been raised knowing that I would go on to college and get an education and reach my potential as a person, because the farther you go, the farther your kids go.
>
> Honestly, I am in love with the person that I have become and I have my parents to thank for that. They are incredible. I'm at the stage where I'm leaving for college in a few weeks for the first time, and I'm going to miss them. It's the end of my childhood and they have made it the best experience of my life so far.[3]

Jonathan, Age 17

Another teen, Jonathan, age seventeen, shares his thoughts on fitting into his adoptive family: "I have no other family to compare my adoptive family to, but my home is a very nice atmosphere. I love my parents and we seem to get along the same way any other family with teens does. Sometimes we have our disagreements, but we get along just fine for the majority of the time."[4] This short quote shares a significant observation that Jonathan has made over the years. He has noticed that families, whether formed through adoption or not, will experience times that are closer than others.

Ben, Age 19

Ben, age nineteen, is one of three adopted children in his family and the only one who is Indian. He shares how the members in his family fit together:

I was born on August 22, 1986, in Calcutta, India, at a hospital called I.M.H. I was adopted four months later in December. When I was born, I weighed only four pounds. Since I became sick and malnutritioned, I soon lost one pound.

I was the last of three kids in my family to be adopted. I have two older sisters who are Caucasian. One is now thirty-four years old with two great kids, and the other is twenty-two years old living in Chicago. Although I am very different from my sisters, I feel like I fit in with my family.[5]

Differences Are Good

All teens, whether adopted or not, can benefit from having different tastes or interests than their friends and family. The very fact that you are different from

Orphan Train

Ticket to a New Family

In the 1800s, changes in the United States caused severe poverty that divided families. The invention of major farm machinery in the early 1800s reduced the need for farmers and caused a flood of people to the city in search of factory jobs. At the same time, hundreds of thousands of immigrants were arriving in American cities looking for work. There were so many workers available that factory owners could pay low wages. Also, because there were so many new immigrants, landlords could charge high rents. Families soon ran out of money, food, and room for their children. Historians estimate approximately 30,000 young children were living on the streets of New York in 1850.

As a result of the poverty, thousands of American children of all ages left their families to find brand-new ones. Homeless children boarded trains called "Orphan Trains" to find a new life. Some were fortunate and found a family that would adopt several children and keep siblings together, but many were separated from their siblings when they were adopted.

The Orphan Trains began running in 1854. They continued to carry children from large cities in the East to new homes in the West and Midwest until 1930. During their many years of operation, these trains carried about 200,000 children to new homes.[6]

others is what makes you interesting. Enjoy who you are. Take pride in knowing you are a one-of-a-kind, unique creation. Your family is special because of its diversities. And it is those differences that often expose you to new ideas and help you try new things. Learn from the different interests and abilities of your siblings and parents. Know that they are learning from you, too. The variety in your family offers everyone new opportunities, not to mention a little excitement.

Teens Ask

Several teens ask questions and voice their concerns about fitting in with their adoptive families in this "Teens Ask" section. Ms. Jenny Spinner offers her advice

> ### ❗ It's a Fact
>
> The book *We Rode the Orphan Trains*, by Andrea Warren, shares the fascinating stories of several orphans and their experiences as orphan train riders. Some of the children had a happy ending with a wonderful family; others were not so lucky. When this book was published in 2001, several hundred orphan train riders were still alive.

on this topic gleaned from years of leading adoption support groups and her experiences as an adopted teen.

My parents adopted me when I was a baby and then they had two biological kids. I have blond hair and my brother's and sister's hair is brown like my parents'. When we meet someone for the first time, they always know who the "adopted" kid is. I love my brother and sister, but sometimes I get jealous because they are my parents' real kids. What should I do?[7]—Jason, age 19

First, let yourself feel jealous. It's okay to feel jealous! Don't judge yourself for how you feel. Don't try and bury the feeling. The danger with burying feelings is that we become cut off from ourselves and the people around us. Jealousy is a natural and instinctive reaction.

When we feel jealous, it generally links in to negative feelings about ourselves, things like not feeling good enough, thinking there is something wrong with us,

> ### ❗ It's a Fact
>
> Ms. Jenny Spinner lives in Bristol, England. She and her two brothers were adopted from different birth families. Her younger sister is the biological child of her adoptive parents. Jenny has worked with Social Services in England and the NCH (National Children's Homes), running support groups for parents on how to help their children work through emotions related to adoption. Jenny belongs to an international peer counseling network called Re-Evaluation Counseling and teaches classes where people learn to counsel each other. She is also involved in presenting workshops for parents and children/teenagers using "special time," an activity that helps build a better parent–child connection. Jenny has traced her birth family and is in contact with her birth mother, brother, uncle, and cousins.

or judging ourselves for feeling jealous. This can make the experience of feeling jealous very painful, but remember that it's not the jealousy itself that's painful, but the feelings that come with it.

Most children are jealous when their parents have more children and there is less attention for them. In a situation like yours, when adoptive parents go on to have biological children, the adopted children can feel a lot of insecurity about their place in the family. They can have feelings about not being with their own birth family. It can emphasize that their own birth mother wasn't able to give them what their adopted mother is giving to her birth children. Young children won't necessarily be making these connections in their head, but the feelings are there all the same. So you can see that the painful feelings that link to the jealousy can be very strong.

Often when parents are busy with a new baby, they don't have time to support the older child in expressing his or her feelings. Either of these things can contribute to the child perceiving it is wrong to feel jealous.

Understanding more about how you felt as a young child can help you understand why you feel the way you do now. It can help you accept yourself more. Do you remember how you felt when your adopted mom became pregnant and then had a baby? And then another one? How old were you? If you don't remember, you could ask your parents how you reacted to having to share them with your two new siblings. They might also have stories about how your next sibling reacted when the youngest was born.

Maybe you could ask your parents to tell you about times they were jealous as children, and even if anything makes them jealous now. If you have a close relationship with your brother and sister, tell them how you feel. Ask your siblings and friends, too. Have a jealousy talk! Of course, people might be too embarrassed to talk about it, but it's worth a try.

If feeling jealous is affecting your enjoyment of life generally, and talking with your family about it is too difficult or doesn't help, then it's a good idea to go to an adoption support group or to get some counseling. If this doesn't feel possible for you at the moment, you could try one thing that helped me a lot with my feelings when I first started exploring them, called "spontaneous drawing." All you need are crayons and some paper. Focus on how you feel for a couple of minutes before you start, and then don't think, just draw and color, picking any crayons you want to use. If you're not experiencing the feelings you want to explore, such as jealousy, at the time, imagine how it feels when you are. You can also focus on yourself at a certain age and then draw.

I feel different from my parents and my brother because they like to do stuff like bike rides, hikes, and snow skiing. My parents always make me go along with them because it's a "family outing." I would rather just stay home. These outings always make me feel like I don't belong in this family. What can I do to stop feeling this way?[8]—Ellen, age 18

I can imagine your many feelings when you are out with your family doing things you don't enjoy. I have a few suggestions, for your family and some for just you, as you try to work through this problem.

First, let's look at the family stuff. You say your parents "make" you go along with them, so I'm guessing you don't feel that you have much say in the matter. I imagine this might leave you feeling that your parents don't listen to you or care about how you feel. This in itself would be enough to make you feel like you don't belong, even if you weren't adopted!

It's common for teens your age to dislike doing some things with their families. Family outings can seem boring compared to spending time with friends or video games. You may even feel embarrassed to be seen doing certain things with parents or siblings. You might be trying to find your own identity that focuses on what you want to do and not what someone else wants you to do. So don't get down on yourself for your feelings.

And feeling unhappy about being out with your family can trigger feelings of not belonging related to your adoption. Studies in recent years are revealing new ideas about adoption and the effects of early childhood experiences. One such theory is that children have an unconscious memory of things that happened to them when they were very young—even as newborn babies. Dr. John Bowlby, one of the leaders in research on the effects of early experiences on the child (and later adult), believes that adopted children may carry feelings associated with being separated from their birth mothers (grief, loss, fear, confusion, anger) that can affect how they feel about themselves and relate to other people. These feelings may be triggered by certain events, which in your case could be when you are out with your family doing things you don't enjoy.

So what can you do? First, understand that parents try their very best to show they love us. I've sometimes noticed that when teenagers try to assert their independence, parents can act a bit funny (e.g., get confused and behave in strange ways) instead of remaining relaxed and loving while you talk things through and try to reach a solution together. It can be useful to understand why they might make rules about having to go on family outings. Ask them why it's important that you go along. You could also ask your parents what their life was like as teenagers. How did their parents treat them? What could and couldn't they do? This might help you understand their behavior towards you.

Arrange a time to talk to your parents about how you feel. Let them know that you want to talk to them in a different way from usual. Tell them you need them to listen to you and ask them to give you plenty of time to speak. You might need someone else there as a support for you to say what you want to say. If it feels too hard to talk to them, try writing a letter to them first explaining how you feel. This might give them a chance to think over what you've said, rather than just reacting from their own feelings.

Another idea is to ask each of your parents to spend some time doing something with you that you want to do. You might want to see a film, bake a cake, listen to music, or play cards. The idea is that they are there to give you attention and support in what you are doing, to enjoy being with you. I call this time parents spend with their teenagers "special time." It's when you get to call the shots and they get to be delighted with you! Doing this regularly can really improve your connection with your parents. For more information on how special time works, read the article about it on Hand in Hand's Parenting website at www. handinhandparenting.org. Look under Articles for "How Special Time Works with Teens." It's really important to get your parents to read this before trying to do it.

As far as family outings, you could try asking members of your family to do something together that *you* like. They might not want to do it, but it's worth a try. Or you could suggest that the family takes turns doing things that each person picks. If there are five people, for example, then every fifth outing would be your choice. Alternatively, you could involve your family in a project to find something that you all enjoy doing. As you think up ideas for an activity, you'll find out more about each other along the way! Part of the project has to be figuring out the best way to go about finding an activity you all enjoy. For example, you could have a big list of all possible activities and then give each a score out of ten, then crossing off the activities that no one likes. This is just one way. Who knows, you might end up having an activities list hanging in the kitchen that people add to over the next week or so.

If your family is interested in learning more about communicating better, I suggest seeing a counselor together or attending family therapy. This will give you a safe environment where you are encouraged to simply be yourself. It will give you more of a chance to find out what being yourself feels like, and your confidence to simply be yourself, no matter how different you are from other people, will grow.

Next, I have some ideas about what you can do with yourself. Explore your feelings around being adopted and belonging to your adoptive family. This can be difficult as feelings are not always easy to get in touch with. So you will probably need help and you'll also need to feel ready. If you don't like the idea of getting counseling or going to an adoption support group, then spontaneous drawing can be a good way to start (see my answer to Jason's question). Writing poetry and stories can be a good way of expressing feelings, too. If you end up crying, let yourself cry for as long as you can. If feelings of anger come up, hit a pillow. Shout if there's no one around, or go for a run. Try letting your feelings out and see how you feel later on in the day. If you feel better, it will give you more confidence to keep exploring letting your feelings out in a way that works for you.

My older sister (who is also adopted) does very well in school and loves it. My parents went to college and think getting good grades is really important. My parents and I fight about homework all the time. School isn't really my thing. How do I make my parents understand I'm different than them?[9]—Eric, age 17

You seem to be comfortable about being different from your family, but frustrated that your parents don't get it. It sounds like it would make a big difference to you if your parents understood how you felt.

It might be helpful to arrange a meeting when you can talk to your parents at a time when they aren't trying to get you to do your homework. Since there is a history of fighting about this issue, having another person there who you trust could help. This person can make sure you have equal time to speak and that you treat each other respectfully. It's a healthy sign when someone in a family realizes help is needed! If it's too difficult to involve another person, at least get your parents to agree to take turns talking. Try to avoid arguing. Often, when situations turn into fights, the underlying issues don't get addressed and communication gets stuck. People end up shouting and saying the same things over and over and no one is listening.

An underlying issue for you could be that you feel very frustrated by having to do something you don't want to do. Unless you feel your parents understand something of what this must be like for you, it's going to be hard for you to listen to anything they have to say. An issue for your parents could be that they are anxious about your future. Unless they feel that you understand something of what this must be like for them, it's going to be hard for them to listen to anything you have to say.

Once you have all really listened to the underlying issues for each other, you may need time to let these sink in before you have another talk to try and address them. It's helpful to take the attitude that your parents want to support you, but they don't always know how. Addressing the concerns they have can make them more open to thinking with you rather than trying to control you. What is their main concern? They might be anxious you won't get a "good" job unless you get good grades. If this is the case, can you address this anxiety? For example, you might be interested in a job that doesn't need good grades. Or a job that doesn't need the type of academic qualifications they are concerned about. Of course, you might not know what sort of job you want to do yet. So consider the fact that if you did end up wanting a job later that needed better grades, would you be prepared to go to night school? Being able to answer these sorts of questions can help to reassure your parents that you are responsible and preparing for your future.

One of your concerns is that you feel you are not being accepted as different. It will help for your parents to understand this and to address it in a way that makes you feel supported. It's very important that differences are acknowledged and talked about in adopted families. If parents try to play down the differences, it can transmit an unconscious message to the child that somehow there is something not okay about being adopted. Sometimes adoptive parents haven't thought very much about the fact that their children might turn out very different from them. Although this also happens in biological families, it can be harder for adoptive parents to accept. Sometimes it can make them feel insecure about being a family, so adoptive parents need to explore these issues with a counselor or each other.

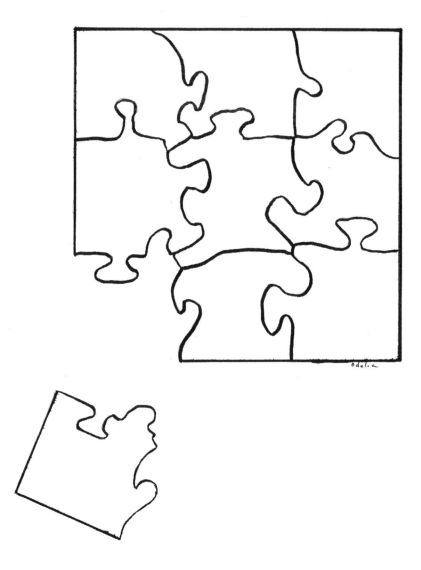

If trying to talk with them goes horribly wrong and you end up fighting, suggest that you see a counselor together. If they resist, explain that homework is well known to cause conflict and stress in families and it's important that some kind of resolution is reached. With the right support, situations that have been "stuck" for years can change overnight.

What about You?

Throughout history parents and teens have found themselves in conflict. Teens around the world wage sibling battles. This type of family strife is universal because the transformation from a child into an adult is not an easy process. Along with major physical changes, you are growing emotionally as well. During your teen years you will very likely experience times when you feel like you don't fit in with your family. Does knowing that family discord and feelings of not fitting in are common teen struggles make them any easier? Perhaps. And maybe some ideas from this chapter, such as acknowledging and recognizing your own special qualities, striving to improve your self-esteem, exploring your feelings about your adoption, opening the lines of communication with family and friends, and seeking outside professional help when needed, can make this difficult time a little easier.

Another helpful activity is to make a conscious effort to stop looking for ways you are different from your family and instead focus on the things you have in common. It's amazing what you will discover when you start looking at a situation with a different purpose in mind. Remember, a puzzle is made with pieces of many different sizes, shapes, and colors, which when put together, create a beautiful picture. You are a unique and special piece in your family puzzle. You fit just as you are, even if the puzzle doesn't create the exact picture you think it should.

Discussion Questions

Do you feel like you "fit in" with your family? Why or why not?

Is there someone in your family that you find particularly hard to get along with? If so, why do you think you struggle with that person?

Do you think being adopted affects how you "fit in" with others at school?

Are there any activities, groups, or sports you've been thinking about getting involved in at school but haven't?

Do you think teens who aren't adopted feel like they don't "fit in" sometimes?

Notes

1. Michael, e-mail correspondence, March 5, 2006.
2. Billy, e-mail correspondence, April 10, 2006.
3. Alanna, e-mail correspondence, March 10, 2006.
4. Jonathan, e-mail correspondence, April 17, 2006.
5. Ben, e-mail correspondence, February 21, 2006.
6. Andrea Warren, *Orphan Train Rider: One Boy's True Story* (New York: Houghton Mifflin, 1996), 14–17.
7. Jason (name changed), author interview, April 23, 2006.
8. Ellen (name changed), e-mail correspondence, December 19, 2006.
9. Eric (name changed), author interview, April 23, 2006.

LEARNING ABOUT YOUR ADOPTION

··

"I was first told about being adopted when I was about six or seven years old, and being young and not able to comprehend a whole lot at that age, it didn't make sense at first. Gradually, my mom was able to talk me through it. I don't remember what I thought at the time, but I know I was confused. I think I cried a little bit (from what my mom said). I wasn't bothered that my birth parents gave me up and I still am not. I know my birth mother died after giving birth because my adoption papers stated that. I'm not sure what happened to my birth father. I have never had the desire to find my birth parents like my sister, Rebecca, did. I figured I have parents I am extremely proud to call my own and they would do anything for me and vice versa. Even almost twenty years old now I still wouldn't change a thing."[1]
—Ben, age 19

Whenever a child is adopted, there is some type of an adoption agreement between the adoptive family and the person or persons placing the child. Just as all adopted persons are special in their own way, every adoption agreement is unique, too. The terms of each adoption scenario can vary greatly, as different states and adoption agencies have their own set of rules that must be followed. The families involved, namely the birth family and adoptive family, usually have input into the adoption agreement as well.

Although an adoption might seem like a personal agreement, it is actually a legal proceeding in which the adoptive parents assume the responsibilities and parental rights for the child. In this process the biological parents legally give up all of their parental rights. An adoption is not "final" until a judge approves the adoptive parents' request to adopt the child. It is very difficult, if not impossible, for birth parents to regain their rights to a child after an adoption is finalized. A legal hearing would need to be conducted, and the birth parents would need to present very convincing reasons why the adoption should be undone. After an

"Parental rights" is a term that encompasses many things. Basically it means that a parent will properly care for a child, providing for his or her physical and emotional well-being. It also means that a parent has the right to make decisions regarding that child. For instance, a parent decides what school or church a child will attend. A parent chooses which doctor or dentist a child should see and when those visits should be scheduled. A parent makes many decisions that affect a child socially, physically, and emotionally. Although parental rights give an adult the ability to decide even small matters, such as if a child may own a dog or hang out with certain friends, a parent never has the right to abuse a child in any way.

adoption is final, it usually stays in effect except under rare and exceptional circumstances.

Types of Adoptions

To gain a better understanding of your own adoption, you must first know some basic information about the different types of adoptions. There are many words used to describe adoptions, such as domestic, international, open, semi-open, closed, traditional, confidential, private, and sealed, and these terms can be confusing. This goal of this chapter is to explain the meaning of these terms and to give you some useful knowledge of the legal system that will help you learn more about your rights and adoption.

Domestic vs. International

First, let's take a look at the geography of adoptions. A domestic adoption is when a child who is born in a particular country is adopted by a family in that same

It's a Fact

Before 291 AD, Roman law stated that only men could adopt children. After 291 AD, women were allowed to adopt if certain requirements, such as death of a biological child, were met.[2]

In 2010, there were about 107,000 children waiting to be adopted from foster care.[3] To grasp that number of people, consider the fact that New York's Yankee Stadium holds about 57,000 people.[4] Now imagine a group of people that would fill the stadium two times—that crowd of people is roughly the number of children in foster care waiting for homes.

A survey conducted in 2002 revealed that about two out of every five Americans have thought about adopting a child sometime in their lives. If you do some math, you will soon discover that around 81 million adults have considered adopting a child. With 107,000 children in foster care, a little over 0.1 percent of the 81 million would need to follow through on an adoption in order to secure homes for the foster care children waiting to be adopted.[5]

country. An international adoption is when a family in one country adopts a child who is living in a different country, usually where he or she was born. Throughout the years, many countries have allowed people from other countries, including the United States, to adopt their children during certain periods of time. At any time and for any reason, foreign countries may open or close their doors for adoptions.

How Open and Who Decides

An adoption is called "open" if there is some type of ongoing contact between the child placed for adoption and the birth family. This contact might include sending letters periodically and/or sharing photos. The amount of openness in an open adoption varies. The type and frequency of contact is determined by the birth parents placing the child, adoptive family, and agency (or lawyer in the case of a private adoption). These specific terms are legally binding and are agreed upon by both the birth family and adoptive family before a child is placed.

In a more liberal open adoption, the birth mother may have a regular time each week or month when she visits her biological child. Some agreements even allow the child to stay at a birth parent's house overnight or for a few days. Sometimes, if a close relationship built on trust develops and both parties are in favor of it, the amount of contact between a child and birth family may increase over time. Open adoptions are becoming more common in recent years. Many adoption professionals believe this situation is beneficial for birth mothers and can also

"I have an open adoption and have known my birth mother ever since I can remember. She visits my family every few years. She's cool, kind of like me. I see her more as a friend than a mother. She didn't raise me like my adopted parents. She wasn't there for me, but she made the right choice in placing me for adoption. I don't think she could have given me what my adopted family has. It's nice knowing my birth mother, because it's like I have a really big family."[6]—Alanna, age 18

result in adopted children with a stronger sense of who they are and where they came from.

Closed Adoptions

A closed adoption, which is also sometimes referred to as a traditional, confidential, secret, or sealed adoption, is an arrangement where there is no contact between the birth family and adopted child. The record of the biological parents is "sealed" and is not available to anyone, including the adopted child. The name of the birth father is often not even recorded on the original birth certificate in a closed adoption. In a typical closed adoption, a second birth certificate is created with the names of the adoptive parents listed as the parents of a child. Today, adoption professionals are recognizing some problems with closed or sealed adoptions. One such issue is that adopted children have no way to access medical information about their birth parents. This information could be critical should certain symptoms or a health condition develop in the child that could not be properly diagnosed due to lack of a medical history.

The novel *Girls in Trouble*, by Caroline Leavitt, is a compelling read about a fifteen-year-old, Sara, who is facing an unplanned pregnancy. After her boyfriend disappears, Sara decides to place her baby girl with a couple in their forties. This book shares the details and complications of the open adoption agreed upon by Sara and the couple, Eva and George. It's a story filled with real emotions that may have you laughing and crying before you're finished.

Semi-open Adoption

Some adoptions are classified as "semi-open." This type of adoption falls somewhere between the traditional (or closed) adoption and the open adoption. A semi-open adoption focuses on maintaining the privacy of all parties

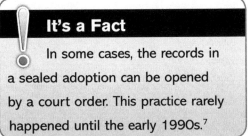

It's a Fact

In some cases, the records in a sealed adoption can be opened by a court order. This practice rarely happened until the early 1990s.[7]

involved, while still allowing contact through a third party such as an agency or attorney. Addresses and phone numbers are not shared, but first names and other nonidentifying information may be exchanged. Many semi-open adoptions include an agreement that specifies the method and frequency of contact, such as allowing the birth mother to send a letter or gifts on the child's birthday or a major holiday such as Christmas. It might also require the adoptive family to send a status letter at set times.[8]

Private vs. Agency

You may have heard people say, "I was adopted privately" or "I was adopted from a private agency." If you've found these types of statements confusing, then read on. An adoption agency is an organization that helps facilitate the adoption of

It's a Fact

Did you know these famous people were adopted?

- Eric Clapton, British singer and songwriter
- Bo Diddley, professional guitar player and important figure in blues and rock history
- Ella Fitzgerald, one of the most famous singers in the world
- Faith Hill, award-winning country singer
- Seal, professional pop singer
- Gerald Ford, president of the United States (1974–1976)
- Nat King Cole, legendary singer and father of singer Natalie Cole
- Nicole Richie, actress and infamous sidekick to Paris Hilton
- Edgar Allan Poe, writer of poems and short stories
- George Washington Carver, chemist and educator[9]

children. Some agencies are sponsored publicly by the State Department. Agencies not affiliated with the government must be approved and licensed by the state before they can open for business.[10] These are often called "private agencies," which is easily confused with a "private" adoption.

A private adoption is when a child is adopted by a nonrelative without agency involvement. In most cases, attorneys, doctors, or a member of the clergy will help couples adopt a child privately. Sometimes, couples advertise their desire to adopt a baby in newspapers and magazines and will locate a child by themselves. Most people who seek to adopt children privately believe they will be able to find a child to adopt much faster than if they worked with an agency. Adoptions through agencies can take up to several years.

Some adoption professionals have expressed concerns about private adoptions because the birth parents often do not receive counseling, as they would from a state-licensed agency. Also, birth parents usually do not seek professional help on their own. Without proper counseling, there is a greater risk that a birth parent will back out on the adoption at the last minute. They also may not be able to process their feelings and loss in a way that will allow them to have an emotionally stable or healthy future. Private adoptions are illegal in some states due to the fact that, unlike public or private adoption agencies, adoption attorneys are not state

Kathleen Hogan Morrison is a Chicago attorney specializing in adoption and parentage matters. Ms. Morrison handles all types of adoption cases, including agency, private, agency-assisted, special needs, related, intercountry, and interstate. She was selected by her peers to be a member of the American Academy of Adoption Attorneys and its board of trustees. Ms. Morrison also served as the chairperson of the Chicago Bar Association Adoption Law Committee and was an expert witness for the Attorney Registration and Disciplinary Commission for the Illinois Supreme Court. She is currently on the Review Committee for the Joint Council on International Children's Services. Ms. Morrison is a frequent speaker and author on issues of adoption, foster parenting, permanency planning, and termination of parental rights.

"Adoption can be a good experience for birth parents, adoptive parents, and their children if the emotional needs of birth parents are met by adoption professionals who understand those needs and know how to meet them. Birth parents making adoption plans out of love and concern for their child's well-being deserve no less than this. Their children deserve early bonding in an excellent adoptive home where there is no fear of disruption."[12]
—Ruth A. Mark, ACSW, Executive Director, Adoption Resource Services

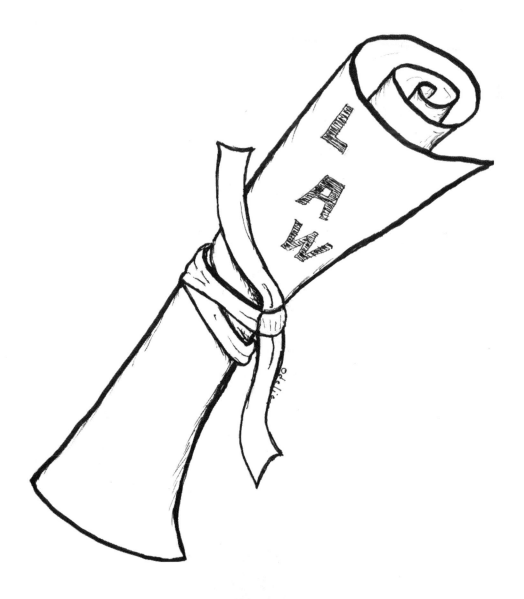

licensed or monitored to make sure the best interests of the birth and adoptive parents, as well as the adopted child, are safeguarded.

Teens Ask

The legal aspects of adoption can be very complicated and intimidating to teens. If the prospect of investigating your adoption seems overwhelming to you, don't despair. Ms. Kathleen Hogan Morrison, an attorney who specializes in adoption law, answered teen questions about accessing adoption records, birth certificates, the legal rights of adopted teens, and how to figure out your adoption type. The information Ms. Morrison shares will give you some basic knowledge about adoption laws and hopefully the confidence to explore your own adoption.

I've heard some adoptions are "open" and some are "closed." How can I find out what kind of adoption mine is?

The terms "traditional adoption," "confidential adoption," and "closed adoption" are intended to mean that the parties will not meet, will not know each other's identities, and will not exchange communications by letter or photograph. In the more modern, or open, adoption, adoptive parents and birth parents will often define for themselves the extent of openness. For example, in some open adoptions, all parties are fully identified by name, address, and telephone number. Biological parents and adoptive parents know each other and communicate. In other, less open adoptions, the parties know each other's first names only and communicate via letter or photograph exchanged through an agency or some intermediary.

Asking your adoptive parents directly is the best way to find out if your adoption is open or closed. If you already have information, background, photographs, letters, and communication from your birth parents, then your adoption is open. If you don't have such information, ask your adoptive parents if they have it. Sometimes parents are unsure how to share information they have. If your adoptive parents have no information because the adoption was closed, you can ask them if it is possible for them to obtain information from the adoption agency or lawyer they used when you were adopted.

Why does my birth certificate have my adoptive parents' names and not my birth parents' names?

You may not know it, but as an adoptee you have two birth certificates. Your original birth certificate sets forth your birth name and date and place of birth, as well

Patricia, an adoptive mother of two teens, shares her thoughts on their open adoptions:

I didn't know what would happen when we agreed to an open adoption, but I knew it was the right thing to do. Now I couldn't imagine doing it any other way. All of our family has a good relationship with both of the children's birth mothers. They are like sisters to my husband, Fred, and me, and loving aunts to the children. Both of them have been unwavering in their support of us and the children. People always ask, "Weren't you afraid they would want the children back?" (which makes both me and the birth mothers giggle) and I answer, "Would your sister take away your child?"

I can't imagine expecting someone who has made the difficult decision to place a child for adoption so that they will have a better future to live without knowing that their child is safe and happy. Both birth mothers tell us almost every time we talk how glad they are that Alanna

The Evans family. From left, Bryant, Alanna, Patricia, and Fred.

and Bryant are with us. I am also glad that the children know their birth mothers so that they know where they came from and where they got some of their talents and characteristics. Alanna got her creativity (art and poetry) and her gorgeous looks from her birth mother and Bryant got a wonderful sense of humor from his.[13]

as the names of your birth mother and possibly birth father. You have another birth certificate that you now use which lists your adopted name, your adoptive parents as your parents, and the date and place of your birth. In most states, the first birth certificate is impounded by the state's Department of Public Health, Division of Vital Records. Adoption records have been impounded and sealed due to traditional ideas that adoption information should be private and secret. The modern approach is to make such information available when the adult adoptee, birth parents, and adoptive parents all agree to the release and exchange of such information.

Can I get a copy of my original birth certificate?

Each state has its own adoption laws. In most states the original birth certificate cannot be released unless all of the adoption triad members agree. For example, if you as a teen want to get a copy of the original birth certificate, you will likely

Laws requiring that adoption records must be sealed began in the early 1900s. The Minnesota Act of 1917 was one of the earliest adoption laws that allowed the children and adults directly involved in an adoption to access their adoption papers. This act prohibited anyone from the general public from obtaining that information.[14] In the years that followed, most of the other states passed similar laws to protect the identity of birth parents from the snooping public. In the 1970s, people began to study the effect of sealing adoption records. The results indicated that some of the psychological issues that many adoptees faced were due to the secrecy that surrounded their adoptions. Open adoptions have become increasingly more common since the 1970s.[15]

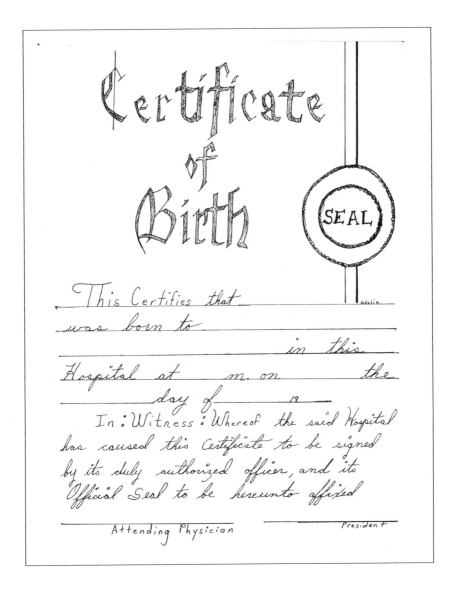

need permission from both your adoptive parents and your birth parents to get a copy. Keep in mind that in many adoption cases, only the Department of Public Health has the document you want. If that is the case, then you have to obey the adoption laws in your state about obtaining copies.

Are there any legal papers from my adoption that would help me find my birth parents?

If you are interested in finding your birth parents, the first thing to do is ask your adoptive parents to show you whatever records they have of your adoption. They may have a Decree of Adoption or Judgment Order of Adoption that identifies your name before you were adopted, as well as when and where you were born.

The document sometimes states the name of birth parents or the name of an adoption agency used in the adoption. The adoption agency may have records about your birth parents. Again, there may be laws in your state that prevent the agency from sharing information with you unless you are twenty-one years of age and your birth parents gave the agency permission to give you information.

Many states have an Adoption Registry operated by the government. If you comply with the state requirements, you may request information and may be able to obtain information from the Registry. Some states require that a Confidential Intermediary (a person authorized by a court to contact birth parents) be employed to do such a search. Adoptees should be prepared for the possibility that birth parents may not be found or have not consented to the release of information or contact.

What legal rights do I have as an adopted teen?

As an adopted teen, you may have the right in your state to request information from the Department of Public Health, a court, or an adoption agency. Most states require that the teen be at least eighteen years of age; some require that the adoptee be twenty-one. If your adoptive parents are supportive of your search, they can often initiate the request for documents on your behalf even if you are too young. In some instances, you will need to wait a few more years before you can do the search you want.

Do my birth parents have any legal rights as my parents?

The parental rights of your birth parents were terminated before or when you were adopted. This means they have no right to be your legal parents. In most states they do have the right to agree or not agree to be contacted by you. This information is often known by an adoption agency or the state Adoption Registry.

It's a Fact

When a child is born in one state and adopted by a family in another state, officials from both of these states must approve the adoption. The 1960 Interstate Compact for the Placement of Children (ICPC), as amended by the Safe and Timely Interstate Placement of Foster Children Act of 2006, spells out the specific guidelines for an out-of-state adoption.[16]

> ## ❗ It's a Fact
>
> Actor Jamie Foxx was adopted when he was seven months old by his grandparents (his mother's parents). Although this famous actor has won a Golden Globe award and an Oscar for best actor, he takes time out of his busy schedule to work as an advocate for adoption.[17]
>
> Jamie has made several appearances on "A Home for the Holidays," the annual musical show presented by the Dave Thomas Foundation for Adoption and the Children's Action Network. This program helps people become aware of the children waiting to be adopted and the need for adoptive families. During its first six years on the air, more than 6,000 people who watched the show called in to receive a packet of information about adoption in the mail. As a result of the show, several children have been adopted.[18]

In some open adoptions, such contact may be direct, face-to-face communication, or communication by letters and photographs. The birth parents and adoptive parents may have a written agreement about what kind of contact will occur in other open adoptions. Such open adoption agreements are only enforceable in court in a few states. In most states, the birth parents and adoptive parents have put in writing their intentions about contact, but the agreement cannot be enforced and ordered by a court.

Did both of my birth parents have to decide to let me be adopted, or just my birth mother?

In every adoption, the parental rights of both the birth mother and the birth father have to be terminated. In many cases where there is a plan for adoption, the birth mother makes the plan and voluntarily relinquishes her parental rights. Although the birth father also has rights, it is sometimes difficult to determine what kind of rights. For example, if the birth parents are married, they have an equal say about any adoption plan. If they are not married, the birth father is called a "putative father," and the extent of his rights vary state by state. In any event, both birth parents should give permission for an adoption plan. There are many instances, however, where the birth father is not involved or has not been identified by the birth mother. If the birth father cannot be located, he may be notified of the pending adoption through newspaper advertising. If he does not

Other State Laws May Apply

"If you were adopted through an agency or attorney in the state where you live, your state's adoption search and reunion laws apply to you. Laws in other states may also govern aspects of your adoption if your adoptive parents adopted from an out-of-state agency or moved after adopting. Adoptees can also be born in one state, adopted through an agency in another state, and live in a third state—so searching for records related to your birth and adoption might encompass several states and be affected by different laws in each state.

"For instance, my sister was born in Wyoming, adopted in Nebraska (when our parents lived there), and raised in Wisconsin. To start her search, my sister needed to contact the placing agency in Nebraska and abide by Nebraska laws in seeking information about her birth parents. To try to find information about her birth (and possibly her birth mother), she had to abide by Wyoming laws concerning the release of hospital records. Most adoptees, in fact, must go back to their placing agency (if it still exists, or to the agency that may have assumed the records from the defunct agency) to start searching for information. The laws in the placing agency's state will determine how the adoptee may proceed."[19]—Ms. Diane Riggs, North American Council on Adoptable Children

contest the adoption, the birth father's rights are terminated, sometimes without his knowledge.

I've tried to find out who my birth parents are but was told I couldn't unlock my records until I'm eighteen. Is that true? If so, why are my records kept a secret from me? And where are these records kept?

In most states, teens under eighteen years of age are denied the right to pursue their birth records. Many states have laws designed to protect the confidentiality and privacy of the birth parents and to shield adoption proceedings from curious bystanders. Most states have chosen eighteen as the threshold age that an adoptee must reach to be considered mature enough to pursue the private details of an

adoption. The age is an arbitrary number chosen by the state legislature as representing adulthood.

Adoption records may be found at an adoption agency, the office of an adoption attorney, the adoption court, or the state's Department of Public Health and/or Adoption Registry. Remember that some records are nonidentifying, which means they may not identify your birth parents by full name or address. Further, some of these records may be incomplete or inaccurate. Consult with your state's requirements about when you may pursue a search and what, if any, restrictions are placed on your search.

Adoption Laws

Some adoption laws are federal, while others are state laws. State laws are only valid for those who live in the state or those who were placed for adoption from

Federal Adoption-Related Statutes

- Adoption and Safe Families Act of 1997, Pub.L. No. 105-89, 111 Stat. 2115 (amended 42 U.S.C. §§670–679 to provide for speedier adoption of foster children)
- Employee Retirement Income Security Act of 1974 (ERISA), 29 U.S.C. §1001, *et seq.* (§§1169(c)(1)–1169(c)(3) (prohibits group health plans from excluding from coverage minor adoptees)
- Indian Child Welfare Act of 1978 (ICWA), 25 U.S.C. §1901, *et seq.* (governs adoption of Native American children)
- Intercountry Adoption Act of 2000, 42 U.S.C. §14901, *et seq.*
- Internal Revenue Code, 26 U.S.C. §1, *et seq.* (§23 establishes the adoption tax credit)
- Servicemembers Civil Relief Act, 50 App. U.S.C. App.2 §501, *et seq.* (governs termination of parental rights by default for parents in the military)
- U.S. immigration law, 8 U.S.C. §§1101(b)(1)(E)–1101(b)(1)(F) (states requirements for intercountry adoption; see 8 C.F.R. §204.3 for related rules)

that state. If you are interested in investigating laws regarding certain adoption topics in your state, see the State Adoption Laws sidebar on the following page to learn various ways you can access state adoption statues. Federal laws are applicable nationwide and are denoted with "U.S.C.," which stands for United States Code. Above is a list of several federal adoption statutes. You can research adoption laws and find answers to your specific legal questions by going to a law library. Law libraries are often located in county, state, and federal courthouses. You can also find adoption laws, or statutes, online.

What about You?

Every adopted person discovers facts about his/her adoption in different ways and at different times. As you mature, you may have new questions that didn't

State Adoption Laws

Adoption laws for each state are found on that state's General Assembly website. To find your state's website, do an internet search using your state name and the words "General Assembly." These sites are designed and maintained by different companies and do not have similar web addresses.

For example, the Illinois General Assembly website is located at www.ilga.gov. California's General Assembly can be found on www.leginfo.ca.gov/index.html. Connecticut's General Assembly website is www.cga.ct.gov. Once you locate your state's assembly site, click on statutes or state laws. Adoption statues usually appear under the category of "family."

Another way to find state adoption statutes online is by going to the Child Welfare Information Gateway website. On the following link, www.childwelfare.gov/systemwide/laws_policies/search/index.cfm, you can choose your state and adoption topic from a provided list, and it will give you the name and number of the applicable statute in your state. For example, the following is a list of some of the adoption laws in Illinois. "ILCS" stands for Illinois Compiled Statutes.

- Adoption Act, 750 ILCS 50/0.01, *et seq.*
- Adoption Compensation Prohibition Act, 720 ILCS 525/0.01, *et seq.* (forbids payment of fees in private adoptions on behalf of biological parents without court order)
- Child Care Act of 1969, 225 ILCS 10/1, *et seq.* (governs licensing of foster care/adoption facilities and homes; creates consumer protection requirements in agency adoptions)
- Children and Family Services Act, 20 ILCS 505/1, *et seq.* (establishes and governs Department of Children and Family Services)
- Contest of Adoptions Act, 750 ILCS 55/0.01, *et seq.* (governs contested adoptions)

- Gestational Surrogacy Act, 750 ILCS 47/1, *et seq.* (creates standards and safeguards in gestational surrogacy contracts)
- Hague Convention of 29 May 1993 on Protection of Children and Co-Operation in Respect of Intercountry Adoption (regulates international adoption of children)
- Health Maintenance Organization Act, 215 ILCS 125/1-1, *et seq.* (§4-9 prevents HMOs from excluding from coverage minor adoptees)
- Illinois Insurance Code, 215 ILCS 5/1, *et seq.* (§356h prevents insurance companies from excluding from coverage minor adoptees)
- Illinois Marriage and Dissolution of Marriage Act, 750 ILCS 5/101, *et seq.* (Part VI, 750 ILCS 5/601, *et seq.,* concerning custody)
- Illinois Parentage Act, 750 ILCS 40/1, *et seq.* (defines the legal relationships of a child born through artificial insemination)
- Illinois Parentage Act of 1984, 750 ILCS 45/1, *et seq.* (governs parentage generally)
- Instruments Regarding Adopted Children Act, 760 ILCS 30/0.01, *et seq.*
- Interstate Compact on Adoption Act, 45 ILCS 17/5-1, *et seq.* (governs placement of special needs children across state lines)
- Interstate Compact on Placement of Children Act, 45 ILCS 15/0.01, *et seq.* (governs placement of children across state lines)
- Juvenile Court Act of 1987, 705 ILCS 405/1-1, *et seq.* (governs abused, neglected, and dependent children)
- Uniform Child-Custody Jurisdiction and Enforcement Act (UCCJEA), 750 ILCS 36/101, *et seq.* (governs interstate child custody disputes)

occur to you when you were younger. It's important to voice your thoughts and pursue your questions. If you want to know more about your legal rights, take the time to locate and read the laws that affect you. Don't be afraid to dig in and get the answers you need. When you learn more about your adoption, you also learn more about yourself. While this is your adoption journey, remember your adoptive parents and many other people care about you and want to help you find the information you seek.

> ## Discussion Questions
>
> What facts do you know about your adoption? (e.g., type of adoption, agency, how old you were)
>
> How did you learn those facts? Did you ask or were you told?
>
> Do you have any questions about your adoption you often wonder about? If so, who do you think might know the answer to your questions?

Notes

1. Ben, e-mail correspondence, February 21, 2006.
2. Christine Adamec and William L. Pierce, *The Encyclopedia of Adoption* (New York: Facts on File, Inc., 2000), xvi.
3. *The AFCARS Report*, September 2010, www.acf.hhs.gov/programs/cb/stats_research/afcars/tar/report18.htm (accessed March 28, 2012).
4. *Yankee Stadium*, www.baseball-statistics.com/Ballparks/NYY (accessed August 14, 2006).
5. *National Adoption Attitudes Survey*, www.adoptioninstitute.org/survey/Adoption_Exec_Summ.pdf (accessed August 14, 2006).
6. Alanna, e-mail correspondence, March 10, 2006.
7. *The Free Dictionary*, encyclopedia.thefreedictionary.com/closed+adoption (accessed February 9, 2006).
8. *Adoption Glossary*, glossary.adoption.com (accessed August 24, 2006).
9. *Adoption.org*, www.adoption.org (accessed April 9, 2005).
10. Child Welfare Information Gateway, "State Laws on Adoption," www.childwelfare.gov/systemwide/laws_policies/state/adoption.cfm (accessed August 24, 2006).
11. Penelope L. Maza, "Adoption Trends: 1944–1975," *Child Welfare Research Notes #9* (1984).
12. Ruth Mark, telephone interview, August 14, 2006.
13. Patricia, e-mail correspondence, April 12, 2006.
14. *Adoption History Project*, "Confidentiality and Sealed Records," www.uoregon.edu/~adoption/topics/confidentiality.htm (accessed August 22, 2006).
15. Adoption Open, "A Brief History of Open Adoption," www.adoptionopen.com/historyofadoption.html (accessed August 22, 2006).
16. *Library of Congress*, thomas.loc.gov (accessed April 9, 2007).
17. Adoption Clubhouse, "Famous People: Artists and Writers—Jamie Foxx," www.adoptionclubhouse.org/02_people/02_artists/03_artist.html (accessed August 24, 2006).
18. Dave Thomas Foundation for Adoption, "A Home for the Holidays," www.davethomasfoundationforadoption.org/programs/a_home_for_the_holidays.asp (accessed August 24, 2006).
19. Diane Riggs, e-mail correspondence, April 9, 2007.

4

WHY DID MY BIRTH PARENTS CHOOSE ADOPTION?

"I have always wondered why my birth mother decided to put me up for adoption. I know that part of the reason is because she was too young to have a child, but I still have many questions. I wonder why she chose my parents and not abortion. I feel lucky, but I would still like to know how my birth mother felt about the whole adoption situation."[1]—Allison, age 17

"**W**hy didn't my birth mother keep me?" is a question that haunts some adopted teens daily, while others may not even give it a second thought. Why is this particular issue more important to some teens than others? It goes back to the same old adage you've probably heard many times—everyone is different, and everyone reacts to certain circumstances and events differently, too.

Who Needs to Know?

There are some adopted teens who, for the most part, feel content with the way things are in their lives. They don't have a burning desire to investigate the past or discover the reasons

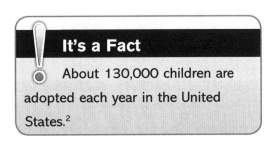

It's a Fact

About 130,000 children are adopted each year in the United States.[2]

behind their birth mother's decision to place them. Perhaps this is because they don't believe these reasons affect their life now or what they will do in the future. These teens often believe that you can't change the past and may view certain events in their lives in a more practical, less emotional way than others.

What about Birth Fathers?

Obviously, every adopted teen has two birth parents—a birth mother and birth father. According to current U.S. laws, both biological parents have the same parental rights for their unborn child. About three-fourths of all teenage pregnancies are unplanned.[3] Babies born under these circumstances account for a significant number of the children that end up being placed for adoption. These teen couples are typically not married and sometimes do not even stay in contact with one another through the pregnancy. It is usually the birth mother, often with her parents' assistance, who makes an adoption plan for her baby. In many adoptions, the birth father is not involved in the decision making at all. His rights are terminated after his child's birth when he does not respond to a legal notice posted in a public forum such as a local newspaper. Because the difficult decision to place a child usually falls on the birth mother, teens and other adoptees tend to focus on their birth mother when they begin to question the reasons behind their adoption.

Other teens may think about their birth mothers quite often. For this group of teens, thinking about the possible reasons why they were placed for adoption is a daily occurrence. And as time goes on, these thoughts seem to be interrupting their lives. At times, they feel an urgent need to search for answers.

Then there are teens who find themselves somewhere between these two ends of the spectrum—between feeling like they desperately need answers and unquestioning acceptance. They may have days when they decide they want to start investigating the facts behind their adoption, but then something comes up that seems more urgent, and in time they forget about the whole thing. Many adopted teens don't necessarily feel a crucial need to know but rather are just curious about why their birth mother did not choose to keep them.

Regardless of how you feel about your past, know that any of these emotions are normal for an adopted teen. And your feelings about this topic will most likely vary through the years. The important thing is to know that whatever you are feeling is okay and to deal with these feelings appropriately. This may mean asking your parents some hard questions, writing a letter to your birth mother,

One of the earliest recorded adoption stories is found in the Bible. The book of Exodus tells the story of Moses, a Hebrew baby who was placed in a watertight basket in the Nile River by his birth mother. The Pharaoh of Egypt had ordered that all newborn Hebrew baby boys be killed. Moses' birth mother was not necessarily thinking of adoption when she put him adrift in the river; she was simply trying to save her baby from certain death. The reason behind her decision is clear—survival for her baby boy.

Moses was later plucked from the river by the Pharaoh's own daughter. She quickly fell in love with the abandoned baby and decided to adopt him. Since bottles and formula were not available back then, a "wet nurse," or woman who was producing milk, needed to feed the baby. Fortunately, Moses' mother had sent his older sister, Miriam, to follow the basket as it floated down the river. Miriam was nearby when Moses' adoptive mother rescued him. On Miriam's suggestion, Moses' biological mother fed and cared for him, allowing Moses the opportunity to bond with his birth mother and adoptive mother alike.[4]

searching for your adoption file, launching a major investigation or whatever else seems right to you.

Teens Ask

Many adopted teens probably wonder about some of these same issues, but don't have anyone they can ask or are afraid to voice them. In this Teens Ask section,

"When I was three months old, my adoptive parents flew from the U.S. to Guatemala City, Guatemala, to adopt me. I don't know much about my birth mother, except that she was eighteen when she had me. The older I get the more I seem to think about her, especially when my friends say things like, "I have the same hair as my mother" or "I am good in music like my mom." I wonder what physical characteristics or talents I have like my biological mother. My whole family is planning to visit Guatemala next year with a tour group of children of all ages who were adopted from there. I hope to learn more about my birth mother, and maybe even meet her."[5]—Liana, age 17

Liana

two birth mothers graciously offered to answer questions asked by an adopted teen named Liana. Hopefully Liana's questions and the answers provided by both birth mothers will help you as you navigate your own adoption journey.

Jamie's Thoughts

Jamie, who placed her baby boy for adoption when she was sixteen, shares her thoughts and feelings on the first two questions about her difficult decision to place her child.

What were the reasons you gave up your baby?

I wanted my baby to have and do all the things that I had and did growing up. I desperately wanted him to have a dad that would love him, guide him, and provide for him. I knew that being only sixteen, I had a lot of maturing and growing left to do. I had to finish high school and figure out college. Education was the only safe plan for any kind of future life. I wasn't sure how I would do all that with a baby and still be the mom I wanted and longed to be. I loved him so much that my fear, hurt, confusion, and many other feelings about letting him go didn't matter as much to me as what would be best for him. I released my baby to adoption so he could have a life that I could not give him.

Did you want to keep your baby?

The minute I found out that I was pregnant, I knew that abortion just wasn't for me and adoption wasn't something that I knew a lot about. The decision to release him to adoption was a long and careful process. I so wanted to keep him. I had all the same feelings that regular moms have. I loved him and wondered and imagined about what he looked like. I felt connected and protective of him while we were sharing my body. I couldn't wait to hold him and tell him that he is loved.[6]

Beth's Thoughts

Another birth mother named Beth, from Colorado, also shared her perspective when she answered a few questions from Liana:

Do you have any regrets about placing your baby?

When I was 14 years old I got pregnant. At first I was sure I would keep my baby. I thought, I can do this; it's no problem. Then I came to my senses and realized

> "Placing a child for adoption may be one of the greatest acts of unselfish love that a person may do throughout a lifetime."[7]—Ruth A. Mark, ACSW, Executive Director, Adoption Resource Services

I needed to find a family to adopt my baby. This was my only option so my daughter could have opportunities that I could not give her. At that time, I was living in an unstable environment. My mom was an alcoholic and drug addict. Fortunately, I was not experimenting with drugs or alcohol and had a very healthy pregnancy. Through my doctor I met Fred and Patricia. They were the first couple I met. It was a true blessing from God to have had them adopt Alanna. They have been a great inspiration to me to be a good mom to the children I have now. Patricia has turned out to be a good role model for me in many areas of my life.

Do you think most birth mothers would want to hear from the children they placed?

I think most birth mothers would want to hear from their children. Open adoption made it possible for me to have a relationship with my daughter, Alanna. Through the years I have had contact with the family that adopted her, the Evanses, and have been a part of their lives. I consider them to be a part of my family. I thank God every day for them being in my life, and for everything they have done for me. One of the proudest moments in my life was watching Alanna graduate from high school. She inspires me to do great things in my life. I know that the people she will meet along the way will be inspired by her also.[8]

Mary's Story: Her Road to Adoption

A birth mother living in Nebraska named Mary offered to share her story of an unplanned pregnancy and how she arrived at the decision to place her baby. Mary wanted to let adopted teens know about her intense and unending love for the baby she placed, hoping it would help them know the strong attachment a birth mother often feels for her child:

> It was one of those late spring days in May with the scent of fresh flowers and new mown grass in the air—not the kind of day you'd like to spend in the doctor's office. But this was where I found myself, trying to figure out what I would do with the positive results Dr. Johnson had just given me.
>
> Having an alcoholic father, I wasn't sure how he'd take the news, knowing how he disliked Tim. Mom would be hurt that she couldn't do

Lisa's Story: Wanting More from a Birth Father

"I was nineteen when I reunited with my birth mother. She was very happy to finally meet me and answered a lot of my questions about her reasons for placing me. I learned that my birth father was getting ready to leave for college when my birth mother became pregnant. They didn't feel marriage was a good option for them at the time. My birth father was anxious to start college. He left before I was born, leaving my birth mother to face a pregnancy and delivery without him.

"As I started developing a relationship with my birth mother, I decided I would like to contact my birth father. My birth mother knew he was a professor at a neighboring state school. She sent him a picture of the two of us together and shared that I hoped to meet him. My birth father had just gotten married and hadn't told his new wife about the fact that he had a child that was placed for adoption many years ago. He quickly returned the picture of me and made it clear he didn't want to meet me, nor would I have a place in his life. I guess my birth father didn't want to risk disrupting his marriage. I think he was also worried that if others in the community found out about me, it would damage his reputation on campus. I felt his response was very selfish, caring more about his life and status than his own daughter. It seemed his reasons for not wanting to be part of my life had not changed since I was born—he was more concerned about his career and reputation than having a relationship with his daughter.

"I also learned that my birth father fought in Vietnam many years ago. I've tried to reason that his war experiences were so traumatic that he is unable to function in a normal or loving way in his relationships. But deep down I realize that's probably not true. I've had to come to terms with the fact that he just doesn't want a relationship with me."[9]—Lisa

anything for me. We usually could talk about anything, even Tim. Tim was a handsome, dark-haired guy with eyes to match. We were unofficially engaged. Christmas was the day we planned to get engaged, but Christmas never came that year for Tim and me. I didn't have much of a chance to talk to him after my parents found out about the pregnancy.

Mary, a birth mother who shares her story, also provided her artwork. This drawing depicts a mother holding her baby.

When I brought up the fact I could be pregnant, Tim said, "What are you going to do about it?"

I replied, "If you don't want me, I'll go away and have it."

"You won't go away with my baby, I'll find you!" he answered.

The next thing I knew, his parents and mine talked. His parents argued that if we stayed together, I would need his money that was set aside for college.

Growing up in the Midwest in the '60s, it was impossible for me to stay home and have the baby. The neighbors knew everything! My two oldest sisters were married. The oldest had three children. My other sister did not have any children yet, and she wanted to adopt my child. Later, she decided not to when she thought about what it would do to me watching my child grow up as my niece. Being Catholic, any other options were not possible.

My father told me, "If you want to keep the baby, you aren't welcome at home anymore." I guess I could have gone away and kept my baby, but back then there was no aid for dependent children and no welfare. I knew I couldn't make enough money to pay for rent and food. I wanted to raise her by myself, but I felt that was impossible without money, a home, and husband. I knew she and I would have suffered, not only from lack of food and warmth, but I'd have to work and be a single parent. So in the end, my parents made all the decisions for me. My parents called the priest to talk about an unwed mother's home near my home. Before I knew what happened, we were on our way there. Many thoughts ran through my mind on that 40-minute drive. *How could my parents do this to me? How could Tim do this to me? Where was he? Did he really care what happened to me and his baby?*

Cabrini Hall was a beautiful, large colonial home. On the outside it looked like a wonderful place to live (with the exception of the thick metal bars on the lower windows). On the interior it was a totally different picture. It was a home for thirty-three girls from all different walks of life, but all with the same situation—pregnant. There was a girl who was pregnant by her stepfather. There also was one who'd been there three times. We were rationed food and could only eat what we were given and only at certain times. The kitchen was padlocked when not in use. We tried to get into it at night to get something to eat. We were allowed to sign out for one hour in the afternoon. The first place we headed was somewhere to get junk food and fruit (sometimes). We had to do chores on our hands and knees until the day we went to the hospital. If it wasn't done to their specifications, we had to do it again.

The entire time I was at the home, my father never came to see me once. My mother, I was told, cried all the time. My sisters would bring Mom to see me once a week. Later I found out Tim did try to find us; first at the home and then at the hospital, but no one would let him in!

Hope and faith were what helped me get through this tough time. I finally went into labor on January 6th. I was dropped off at the back door of the hospital alone. I could hear others who were in labor, with their family or husbands. I got to hold my baby daughter twice. When I held her the last time, I told her we'd meet again whether in heaven or on this earth. It was as if she knew what I said as she looked up at me with her dark eyes. I looked at her and just felt so much love for this little baby who had spent nine months growing in me. I didn't know if I would have the strength to give her to someone else to love. I wanted so much to keep her, but I knew that I couldn't. I had thirteen days in which to make up my mind on what I would do; adoption or to keep my baby.

When the adoptions papers were placed in front of me, I felt as if someone cut my heart out and told me to go on living without it. They told us that the child would not be placed in the same town or same state in some cases, but I later found out this was not true in our case. We had probably crossed paths at the grocery store. My main concern with the adoption was to give my baby a secure, warm, and loving home with a mother and a father. I knew this was something that she and I would never have with Tim.

Mary's Postscript

"For many years after I placed my daughter, I would write Catholic Social Services to tell my caseworker where I was, even after I married a wonderful man

The flight of a Butterfly freedom
the Smell of a Rose Peacefulness

Art by Mary. The butterfly symbolizes the freedom a birth mother is giving to her child when she places that child with a loving family. The rose in the drawing stands for the hope of peace for both the child and birth mother.

Imagine a Moment

Just imagine a moment you found your only daughter,

that you thought you'd never again see.

She is so sweet and charming,

and much like you wanted to be.

You didn't want to give her up, but had no other choice,

because at that time you felt that you never had a voice.

In her life you'd always hoped you'd be.

What a sweet baby, but now she's let free.

To be a person, a someone to somebody.

To make her life a special one,

not just a child on the run.

The adoptive parents gave her all I'd hoped to give,

so that my dear sweet baby would have a chance to live—

Her life, not for just one moment, but forever and a day.

Even though she'll never share his or my name,

But like us just the same, she'll have his brown eyes,

my smile, maybe my walk,

or maybe even the way that I talk.

Dreams are for imagining, but somehow this one came true,

I met my only daughter and now she has a daughter too!

(Written by Mary about the daughter she placed for adoption)

named Jerry and God blessed me with two sons. I told both boys about their sister when they were ten and fourteen. The oldest was a little hurt that he wasn't my first child as he had thought, but when he realized that I needed to bring peace to my life, he accepted all of this.

"I received a letter from the adoption agency saying my daughter was seeking information when she was nineteen, but then I didn't hear anything else for awhile. I tried to find her by writing the area newspaper, the doctor's office from the home, and the attorney from the home, but no one would help me. When I had almost given up, I received a call. The voice on the other end said, 'I think I have your daughter right here by my side!' My heart came up in my throat!

Drawing by Mary

"When we did meet, we grabbed each other and hugged as if we'd never been apart. I just wanted to be with her all the time, but I had to hold myself back. I had to let her make the first moves. I could not hurt this special relationship we had gotten back by some miracle. And I could never hurt her adoptive parents. They were the ones who went through all the growing pains with her. I didn't have the

Mary (left), reunited with her daughter, Lisa (at age 20)

times with the upset tummy, first tooth, the first prom, or the wedding day. They had all of those things with her. And they did everything for her that I couldn't. My life is so complete and so blessed with her in it now. I now know that my God loves unconditionally. I know this because he placed my daughter back in my life."[10]

Every Situation Is Different

The circumstances leading to the decision to place a baby for adoption are very special and unique for each birth mother. The reasons your birth mother placed you will be very different from the adoption scenario of another teen. As a teenager it may be difficult for you to comprehend that there are any valid reasons for a birth

Birth mothers today have many more options than they did just a few decades ago. In the 1960s, unwed mothers were shunned and looked down upon. They were often sent off to live in a maternity home until their babies were born. These homes were generally sponsored by a church or religious organization. The birth mother's family wanted to avoid the embarrassment of having their pregnant daughter seen around town. Once the child was born, their daughter would return home and everyone would pretend that nothing ever happened.

But these young teenage mothers could not deny the strong feelings they had experienced for their babies or the anger they felt over having no control over their situation. In 1968, a seventeen-year-old named Nancy Horgan was sent to Sophia Little Home in Rhode Island when she was seven months pregnant. For two months Nancy did crafts with the other young expectant mothers that lived there. She was not prepared to give birth or for the overwhelming emotions she would experience after her baby was born. Nancy repeatedly asked the hospital staff to let her hold her newborn son, but her request was never granted. She was allowed to briefly see him once through the glass window in the nursery. Twenty-one years later, Nancy went searching for her son. When she met Kurt for the first time, she shared that she had never been allowed to even touch him. The meeting brought up past feelings of regret and anger for Nancy, who then sought the help of a psychiatrist to help her deal with those issues. Kurt and his birth mother, Nancy, share a positive and close relationship today.[11]

Off the Bookshelf

In the novel *Find A Stranger, Say Goodbye*, by Lois Lowry, a seventeen-year-old girl named Natalie Armstrong begins to have questions about her adoption during her senior year in high school. Natalie finds herself lying awake at night, unable to stop wondering why her birth mother decided not to keep her. Constantly bombarded by feelings of anger, sadness, and confusion, Natalie feels as though she is riding an emotional roller coaster. Finally, Natalie asks her adoptive parents for their help in searching for her birth mother. Natalie's parents give her a box that contains all the information they have about her birth family. With just a few cryptic clues, Natalie begins her search. Although she doesn't find the birth mother she had envisioned, Natalie finds the answers she needs, and is satisfied with the details she uncovers as she learns the facts about her own adoption story.

mother not to keep her child. Perhaps, living in a comfortable home where your parents have provided well for you and life seems rather easy, you might mistakenly think that raising a baby is not that hard. Until you become a parent, you will never fully understand the time, energy, money, commitment, and help from family and neighbors it takes to care for a baby properly. If you find yourself struggling with these types of thoughts, you might consider spending some time with a mother who has a new baby. You could also volunteer to help out in the church nursery or lend a hand to a neighbor with several kids. There's nothing like firsthand experience to help you understand how a person who is in a situation that is unknown to you might feel.

Some Reasons Why

There are various reasons birth mothers choose to place a child. To try and list them all here would be impossible. But it might be helpful for you to spend some time considering some of the most common ones.

Too Young

A very young birth mother may decide adoption is the best alternative because she knows she is not ready to become a parent. She may realize she is not mature

> ## ! It's a Fact
>
> Before 1972, a birth father who was not married to his child's birth mother had no legal rights to the child. If a birth mother decided to place the child for adoption, the birth father could not alter her decision. He also had no paternal rights after the child was born.
>
> All this changed in 1972 when the case *Stanley v. Illinois* was heard in the U.S. Supreme Court. Peter Stanley, who was not married to the mother of his children, won custody of his three biological children and also paved the way for birth fathers to gain new rights.[12]

enough, nor emotionally ready to handle the responsibilities of caring for a new baby. Perhaps she hopes to finish high school and even go on to college. A birth mother may even recognize that she is still a child herself and she wants to grow up before she becomes a parent.

Financial Insecurity

Birth mothers, especially those who are young, may be unable to pay for the essentials such as housing, food, or clothes for their child. Even in today's world, where welfare benefits are available to mothers with dependent children, birth mothers may want their child to have more than the poverty-level existence they could provide. Some birth mothers dream of their children having simple luxuries that they may have never experienced, such as their own room, extra food in the pantry, private music or dance lessons, or a college education.

Two Is Better Than One

Many unmarried birth mothers come to the conclusion that adoption is the best option because they want their child to have two loving parents. They believe this decision will give their baby the benefit of an involved, caring, and nurturing father. Perhaps a birth mother hopes her child will have a loving father, just as she did, or the type of father she wished she would have had. A birth mother often tries to imagine her child's future. She may picture her child developing a close and healthy relationship with a father who takes the time to go fishing or play ball in the yard. Birth mothers often dream of their children growing up in a stable home with two loving parents.

Bad Scene

A birth mother who lives in a dangerous situation, for example, one that might include drugs, alcohol, or an abusive environment, may place her baby for adoption to protect her child. Sometimes this mother-to-be does not have the means to escape her current living arrangement or unstable family members. And the sad truth is that some birth mothers are battling an addiction themselves and know they are unable to care for a child. Certain health issues, such as depression, anxiety, or psychological problems, may also cause a birth mother to choose an adoptive home for her baby. In some instances, a birth mother may even be battling serious, life-threatening disease and does not have the strength or energy to care for a baby.

Beyond Her Control

Some birth mothers find themselves in circumstances beyond their control that force them to place their child. Some foreign countries have government policies that do not allow them to keep their babies. China, for example, has enforced a

In November 2006, the Evan B. Donaldson Adoption Institute published an eye-opening report titled "Safeguarding the Rights and Well-Being of Birthparents in the Adoption Process," which provided some much-needed, up-to-date information about the background and wishes of birth mothers. This study, written by Susan Smith, revealed that only one-fourth of the birth mothers involved in recent adoptions were in their teen years. In fact, most birth mothers were in their twenties and had graduated from high school, and many were raising other children.

Smith's work also reported that birth mothers were very involved in the process of choosing adoptive parents for their children. This study estimated that over 90 percent of birth mothers had met the adoptive parents of their children and that nearly all of the remaining 10 percent helped to select the parents who adopted their children. Another finding in Smith's study indicated birth mothers have a strong desire for openness in their adoptions. The report stated, ". . . almost no women choosing adoption today seek anonymity or express a desire for no ongoing information or contact."[13]

"one-child" policy for many years. As unbelievable as it may seem, thousands of women in China do not feel they have the option of keeping their second child.

Parental influence may cause some young birth mothers to feel like they have no choice other than adoption. Many parents, who believe they are acting in the best interest of their daughter, may require their daughter to place her child if she wants to remain living at home.

What about You?

If you feel a deep need to know why your birth mother decided on adoption and find this issue is overtaking your thoughts, then perhaps this question is worth pursuing. Learning about your birth mother's situation and her reasons for choosing adoption will most likely help you move past this question and get on with your life.

As a woman with an unplanned pregnancy thinks about the options that lie before her, there is one prevailing reason that causes most birth mothers to choose adoption—love. Although she has never seen or held her unborn child, this love is very real and tangible. It is a love that is difficult to understand or put into words. As surely as a birth mother's baby has continued to grow for nine months, so has her love for the child she has carried with her wherever she goes. But sometimes circumstances and other factors in life cause a birth mother to make a decision that can later be questioned or misunderstood by her child. This child may feel rejected or abandoned, when the true motivation for the adoption was love and hope for a wonderful future.

In the year 2000, the United States Postal Service issued a 33-cent stamp that celebrates adoption. The stamp was designed by Greg Berger, an adoptee from Bethesda, Maryland. The center of the stamp contains a colorful, contemporary picture of two people holding hands outside a home with the words "Adopting a CHILD. Creating a WORLD. Shaping a LIFE. Building a HOME." lining the edges.

A ceremony in the Beverly Hills post office was held May 10, 2000, when the stamp was first issued. Dave Thomas, along with stars such as Henry Winkler, Paula Poundstone, and Rhea Perlman, attended the event. The stamp encouraged families to consider opening their homes to a child through adoption. Although the stamp is no longer available for purchase, it helped spread the word about adoption when it was in circulation.[14]

A birth mother longs for her baby to have the best life possible. Most birth mothers consider the needs of their child over their own desire to keep the child. Placing a child for adoption is an unselfish, caring, and mature decision that is often very painful to make. It's important to remember as an adopted teen that you are twice loved, first by your birth mother and then by your adoptive parents.

Discussion Questions

What are some of the reasons you think birth parents choose adoption for their children?

Does anyone in the group want to share their birth parents' situation and why you think they made an adoption plan?

What are some things you appreciate or like about your adoptive family?

How might your life be different if you had not been adopted by your family?

Notes

1. Allison, e-mail correspondence, September 7, 2006.
2. Child Welfare Information Gateway, www.childwelfare.gov/pubs/s_adopted/s_adopteda.cfm (accessed April 10, 2005).
3. Ross Werland, "How Young Minds Plan Pregnancy," *Chicago Tribune*, September 3, 2006, 8.
4. Exodus 2:1–10 (New International Version).
5. Liana, author interview, August 26, 2006.
6. Jamie, e-mail correspondence, May 12, 2006.
7. Ruth Mark, telephone interview, August 14, 2006.
8. Beth, e-mail correspondence, April 25, 2006.
9. Lisa, author interview, September 6, 2006.
10. Mary, e-mail correspondence, October 2, 2006.
11. "Forced to Give Up Their Babies," *People* (September 18, 2006), 159.
12. Christine Adamec and William L. Pierce, *The Encyclopedia of Adoption* (New York: Facts on File, Inc., 2000), 51.
13. Susan Smith, "Safeguarding the Rights and Well-Being of Birthparents in the Adoption Process," Evan B. Donaldson Adoption Institute (November 2006), www.adoptioninstitute.org/publications/2006_11_Birthparent_Study_All.pdf (accessed February 5, 2007).
14. "Adoption Stamp," www.westsidechildrens.org/news/archive/article12.html (accessed September 5, 2006).

5
SHOULD I SEARCH?

"I've never met my birth mother and think it might be a good thing to meet her, and in the same respect it might not be. I have no hard feelings or anything of that matter, although sometimes I wonder who she is and what she's doing at times. Sometimes I wonder how my birth parents would accept me. How would they react if I said, 'Hi, I'm your son that you gave up for adoption.' And how would I react to them. Would it be better not to meet them because it could be very awkward? Would they want to see me after I've invested all that time to find them?"[1]
—Jonathan, age 17

Should I try out for the soccer team?
Should I cut my hair or grow it long?
Should I study for my final exam or blow it off?
Should I order a hot fudge sundae or get a banana split?

As a teen, you make many decisions every day. And with each decision comes certain consequences in your life. For example, if you decide to try out for the soccer team, you might be chosen for the team, have the opportunity to improve your skills over the years, and wind up getting a college scholarship to play soccer. On the other hand, you may be setting yourself up for a major disappointment if you don't make the team. If you decide to get a haircut, you might love your new look, but your boyfriend may hate it. If you study hard for your final, you might ace the class, boost your GPA, and open up new options for colleges.

> "I have tried to search for my birth mother and found a few pictures. My adoptive mother has written my birth mother letters, but I have not heard back from her. I would love to hear from my birth mother or at least talk to her. I have also thought about trying to visit her, but I think it would be better to try that a little later, when I mature."[2]—Michael, age 17

If you choose to hang out at the mall instead of study, you may flunk the class and have to take it again next year. If you chose the banana split over the hot fudge sundae, you would spend 50 cents more and gain a little extra potassium. You get the idea—some decisions require more thought than others. The possible consequences from some decisions will have a greater impact on your life than others.

But what about the unique decisions you face as an adopted teen? The question of whether or not to search for your birth mother or birth parents can be a very complicated issue. It's a decision that your parents, good friends, and a counselor can help you think through, but in the end, it's one that only you can make. Every adopted person must decide if, and when, he or she will go searching for a birth parent.

What's in My Genes?

There are many reasons adopted people want to search for their birth family. A common one is simple curiosity about heredity. Teens often wonder about the genetic characteristics they may have inherited from their biological parents. It's not unusual for adoptees to want to find out if they look like their birth mom or dad. Knowing your biological background may help explain why some subjects in school come easier to you than others. Genetics may also play a part in your ability to excel in certain sports or why you are a total klutz in activities that require good hand–eye coordination. Although finding out your genetic history won't really change your abilities, it might help you discover some new avenues to explore that you might not have thought of trying before.

Medical History

You also may be interested in searching for your birth parents in order to obtain your medical history. This can be invaluable information to help diagnose or prevent certain health conditions. For example, if one of your biological

(c) C Papile 1995

parents suffers from a health problem that is often hereditary, such as diabetes, certain types of cancer, or asthma, you are more likely to recognize the early symptoms of these diseases because you may be looking for them. Or if you develop some type of medical problem that your doctor is unable to diagnose, your medical history may provide the clues he or she needs to figure out exactly what you have.

Learning Disabilities

Another aspect of medical history that can be very important for teens to learn about is learning disabilities or development problems that have occurred in their family. The phrase "learning disability" is used to describe when a person's brain works differently than others because of a neurobiological disorder. People with learning disabilities generally have average or above-average intelligence, but their performance, particularly in schoolwork, is usually below average.[4]

About half of all learning disabilities, attention deficit/hyperactivity disorder (ADHD), and language or motor skills problems are passed genetically from parents to their children.[5] Adoptive parents are often unaware of certain learning issues in their child's biological family and therefore may have difficulty recognizing learning problems in their adopted children. Another problem is that some symptoms of learning disabilities can be misdiagnosed as a completely different problem. For example, a child with ADHD may exhibit symptoms that are similar to a very different disorder called reactive attachment disorder. Information about biological parents could be crucial in making a quick and accurate diagnosis.

Carol Barbieri, an adopted woman living in New Jersey, found out the importance of knowing her medical history during a sudden medical emergency of her child. When Carol's fourteen-year-old son displayed symptoms of what could be a serious heart condition called Wolff-Parkinson-White, his doctor needed to know if anyone else in the family had been diagnosed with this rare disease. The answer to that question would determine if Carol's son should have a high-risk corrective surgery immediately or not.

Unfortunately, Carol did not have her complete medical history or access to that information. Her adoption records were sealed, and it would require time-consuming legal action to open them. Time she and her son didn't have. As her son's condition stabilized, Carol set out to obtain her medical information any way she could. It was a matter of life or death for her son. In her search, Carol openly admits she lied, broke the law, and pretended to be other people. In her quest for answers, Carol stopped at nothing to help her son. Eventually she tracked down her birth family. She found she had five siblings, all of whom displayed no heart problems.

Carol's son ended up having three heart surgeries, the last of which was very successful. He enjoys good health today. Carol later discovered that she had a second cousin who died of a heart problem that doctors suspect was Wolff-Parkinson-White syndrome. Perhaps Carol's cousin would not have died if he had been aware of Carol's son's condition.

After experiencing so many difficulties in obtaining her medical records, Carol wrote an article that appeared in the *New York Times* on November 29, 2005, which alerted the public to the need for a change in New Jersey legislation. Carol hopes that New Jersey will pass a proposed bill that will give adopted adults in that state the right to obtain a copy of their original birth certificate.[6] This single document contains vital information which can lead to discovering a medical history or meeting birth parents. If the proposed adoption legislation passes in New Jersey, this state will join seven others—Alabama, Alaska, Delaware, Kansas, New Hampshire, Oregon, and Tennessee—that currently allow adopted persons access to their records.[7]

> **It's a Fact**
>
> Attention deficit/hyperactivity disorder (ADHD) is a frequently diagnosed behavioral disorder in children today. Children and teens with ADHD suffer from a variety of symptoms, such as an inability to stay focused on the task at hand (like schoolwork), difficulty in responding to others in a timely manner, a tendency to fidget or an inability to sit still, and impulsive actions that can lead to social problems. While scientists and medical professionals are still unclear about the specific cause of this disorder, studies have shown that it is often hereditary. If an adult is affected by ADHD, his or her child has a 57 percent chance of also having this disorder.[8] It has been shown statistically that adopted children have a higher incidence of ADHD than children who were not adopted.[9] A great resource for people with ADHD is an organization called Children and Adults with Attention Deficit/Hyperactivity Disorder, more commonly referred to as CHADD. You can visit their website at www.chadd.org for more information.

Finding Out the Real Reasons

Many teens feel a need to search for their birth parents to find answers to various questions they have. They may feel rejected or that they weren't "good enough" to keep. Perhaps you share some of those thoughts. If so, you may need to know exactly why your birth mother did not keep you, so you can eliminate your fears and irrational thoughts. Finding out the real reasons your birth mother decided that adoption was the best plan for you can be helpful if you struggle with feelings of low self-worth.

Is My Birth Mother Okay?

You may be perfectly content with the fact that your birth mother made the decision to find another couple to be your parents. In fact, you might be very happy she did, because you can't imagine having any other parents than your own. But you still may have concerns and fears about your birth mother. *Is she okay? Does she regret placing me? Is she lonely, poor, sad, or homeless?* These types of fears are common for some adopted teens. Sometimes these concerns become so strong that an adopted teen feels an urgent need to make sure his or her birth mother is doing well.

What Am I Missing Out On?

Another common fantasy that teens create is that their birth mother or birth father is a very wealthy or famous person. Teens may fantasize that their birth mother is a popular rock singer or their birth father is a famous movie star. When the going gets rough, some teens like to imagine how perfect their lives would be if they were reunited with their overly cool and super-famous "real" parents.

Perhaps you haven't wondered about having famous birth parents, but your reason for wanting to search is to find parents that understand you. You envision parents that don't make ridiculously early curfews or other seemingly unfair rules, like your adoptive parents. While this reason may be a driving factor to lead you to search for your birth parents, just keep one thing in mind. If a parent truly loves a child, that parent will do whatever it takes to protect that child and keep him or her safe. Sometimes this means enforcing rules, even if it makes their child angry at the time. Being a good parent is not a popularity contest. Parents make rules and decisions that they feel are best for their children and will keep them out of harm's way.

Am I Ready?

Creating a shopping list is a great way to be prepared when you go to the grocery store or hit the mall. One of the best ways to determine if you are ready to launch a search for your birth parents is also to make a list. By writing out all of the events that could happen during your search, you can organize your thoughts and visualize the possibilities ahead. Listing the best and worst things that may occur if you go looking for your birth parents will help you think about potential scenarios that could unfold and help you decide if you are prepared to handle these situations.

Below is a sample list of best- and worst-case scenarios that might happen when an adopted teen searches for a birth parent. You can use this list, add to it, or create your own.

Search Possibility List

Best

- Your birth mother is easy to find.
- You can easily locate your birth father, too.

- You are able to e-mail or write your birth parents, so you can get to know them before you meet them.
- When you meet your birth parents, everyone involved (such as your adoptive parents and siblings) immediately likes one another and no one feels threatened.
- Your birth mother is a famous singer and she wants you to go on tour with her.
- You birth father is unbelievably wealthy and he gives you millions.
- None of the members of your birth family have any physical or mental problems.
- Your birth family becomes part of your extended family, just like family members who live far away and you really enjoy seeing when you get the chance.
- You discover you have siblings and you get along great.
- Your mom and birth mom really like each other, and you don't feel caught in the middle.
- You stay in touch, but not so often that the contact feels intrusive in your life.

Worst

- You can't find your birth parents.
- You find them and they don't want to see you.
- You discover one, or both, of your birth parents are dead.
- You birth parents are unstable or addicted to drugs.
- Your birth mother decides she wants to be your mom—even though that job is already taken.
- Your birth mother has other children, but you're the only one she placed.
- Your learn your birth parents tried to abort you.
- Your birth parents are married, but your dad did not want to keep you.
- You don't like your birth parents.
- One of your birth parents is in jail.
- Your birth parents don't care about you.
- Your birth parents are in financial trouble and try to get money from you.

After you have made your list, you can discuss each item with a mature friend, an adult you trust, or your parents. You might ask others to add their ideas to your list of best- and worst-case scenarios. Talk about how you would handle such situations and ask their advice.

Of course, keep in mind the list you created contains the very best and worst options. Chances are your search will end up with situations that are somewhere in between. For instance, perhaps it isn't easy to find your birth mother, but after a long search you are able to locate her. When you meet your birth mother you find that you don't have a lot in common, but you don't particularly dislike her either. She just seems like any one of a number of people that you have met for the first time—rather pleasant and (gasp!) somewhat ordinary. And while you may have expected a very emotionally charged meeting where you find out she is the most loving, interesting, exciting, and fabulous person in the whole world, instead you have a rather tame, congenial reunion where you discover she cares about you very much but is a real person with flaws and issues just like everyone else.

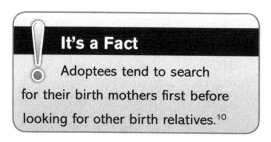

It's a Fact

Adoptees tend to search for their birth mothers first before looking for other birth relatives.[10]

My Story: Lisa

When Lisa was a freshman in college, she decided it was the right time for her to search for her birth mother. At the age of nineteen, Lisa embarked on this journey by herself. After a lengthy search, Lisa discovered two clues that eventually led her to her birth mother:

Growing up, my family didn't openly talk about adoption. I was around five or six when my parents told me I was adopted, but we didn't discuss it much after that. For some reason the subject seemed "taboo." I thought it would hurt my parents' feelings if I brought it up, so I rarely did.

Once I hit my teen years, things got hard. I wanted to break away from my parents in some ways and gain a little independence. As time went on, I felt the need to know where I came from and why I was like I was. After I left home for my first year at college, I decided it was time to launch my search.

I called the adoption agency that had placed me and told them I wanted to meet my birth mother. They responded that I wasn't old enough to get any identifying information without my parents' permission. (I was nineteen, and I needed to be twenty-one.) I didn't want to involve my parents, so a few weeks later I drove to the agency to see what nonidentifying information they would give me. They had a box full of stuff about my adoption, but I was only given two items.

I received a letter from my birth mother and a "Birthparent Questionnaire" form she had filled out. The agency had contacted my birth mother and obtained both when I called them a few weeks earlier. The three-page letter began "Dear Daughter." In the first line my birth mother apologized for the informal greeting, and shared that she had named me Laura when I was born. At the end of the letter I learned my birth mother shared my dream that we could meet. I reread her letter again and again. It helped me get an idea of what kind of person she was. Unfortunately the agency had removed the phone number she supplied. In her letter she wrote, "Please call me if you want to, [number deleted], or write. I want to hear from you so much, or even to just get a picture of you. I also would like to meet your Mom and Dad. I do hope some day God will let me meet you." It made me angry that although both my birth mother and I wanted to contact each other, the agency intentionally kept us apart.

The six-page questionnaire contained some basic facts about my birth mother, such as her height, weight, eye color, hair color, and birthday. Almost half of the form was dedicated to my medical history on my birth mother's side, which didn't provide any information that seemed significant. It also had a section which asked her to describe her current family situation. I learned my birth mother married after she placed me, and I had two half-brothers, ages seventeen and thirteen. It seemed strange to think that I had brothers somewhere that I'd never met.

I kept searching the questionnaire, hoping to find clues that would help me find my birth mother. Then I saw her place of employment, The Tannery. Bingo! Even though the social workers at the agency had been kind enough to share that my birth mother now lived in Nebraska, I didn't think that was enough to go on. Then I found another word that I thought would help me solve the mystery—Wandel. That name appeared on the corner of one of my half-brothers' pictures in very tiny letters. I realized it must be the name of a photo studio. It didn't take me long to find a town in Nebraska with The Tannery and a Wandel studio.

I decided to call the tanning salon and pose as a customer. I explained to the woman on the phone that I had been in that week and a very nice woman had helped me, but I couldn't remember her name. My heart was racing as I provided a description of the woman, straight from the birth mother questionnaire—5'3" tall, about 120 pounds, blue eyes, brown hair . . . and the woman promptly responded, "Oh, that has to be Mary." I thanked the woman and quickly hung up. I had a name—Mary. But I wasn't ready to do anything with it just yet. I needed time to compose myself. Time to understand the new emotions that were suddenly and unexpectedly welling up inside me. I was unsure and scared. And I also knew I needed to talk to my parents before I contacted Mary.

I soon shared the details of my search with my parents. It was very difficult for me to tell them that I had done this behind their backs. At first they were devastated. It was the first time I ever saw my Dad cry. He wasn't mad, he was just confused and hurt.

"Did we do something wrong?" he asked through his tears. "Is what you have not enough?" he pressed. I gave my parents the letter my birth mother had written, and then I gave them time. I waited a whole month. I wanted the idea of reunion with my birth mother to begin to sink in.

At the end of that month, I called The Tannery again and asked for Mary. I was ready to know if this woman was my birth mother. When Mary came to the phone, I began my well-rehearsed speech. "My name is Lisa. I've been in contact with Catholic Social Services in Peoria. I was born on January 6. Did you have a daughter at St. Francis hospital that you gave up for adoption?" My question was met with complete silence. Neither one of us said a word for several minutes, but we both knew what that silence meant. My search was over! Then we both broke down and cried. Separated by hundreds of miles, we sobbed together. When we could finally speak, we decided that Mary would fly to meet me.

Lisa (left) and her birth mother, Mary (right). They are hugging Lisa's daughter, Karley.

A few weeks later Mary flew into the airport near my home. My parents went with me to pick her up. Mary's parents and sisters lived near my hometown, so they also had gathered at the terminal to wait for Mary's plane. The main thing I remember about that day was watching my mother sitting in a chair at the airport crying. I wanted to sit beside her and comfort her, yet I also wanted to focus my attention on the woman who had given birth to me nineteen years ago. I felt very torn. After brief and tearful introductions at the airport, everyone drove back to my parents' house.

We talked and took lots of pictures. The gathering seemed awkward the whole time. I felt I needed to keep both my parents and birth mother happy, but I wasn't sure how to do that. After our meeting, Mary and I kept in touch by writing and calling occasionally.

Over the years our relationship has been like a roller coaster ride. We would go through periods when we are close, and then other times when our relationship is strained. Big events, like major holidays, my graduation, and my wedding were especially difficult. It was always in the back of my mind that Mary's presence may upset my parents. Since I met my birth mother, I feel like I'm always trying to keep the peace.

My birth mother and I now enjoy a very comfortable relationship. I don't call her Mom because we don't have the typical mother–daughter relationship. We have more of a friendship and I'm glad that I found her. I love her and I know she will always love me.[11]

> "Knowing what I know now, I really wasn't mature enough or emotionally ready to meet my birth mother when I was nineteen, but I don't regret it."[12]—Lisa

Teens Ask

Allison, an adopted teen, was placed with her family when she was only three days old. Her adoptive parents did not use an agency but adopted her privately. Allison's adoptive grandmother was an acquaintance with her birth mother, and the adoption was arranged through that relationship. Even though Allison's family had a connection to her birth mother many years ago, Allison does not have any information about where she might be now. She does not know her birth mother's name. In recent years, Allison has become more curious about her birth mother and wonders if she should begin searching. As she weighs her options, Allison has two questions she would like answered as she goes through her decision-making process.

Allison

Do you think my birth mother would want to hear from me?

Allison, the answer to this question may be a little more difficult to find out since your adoption was private. Birth mothers typically make their wishes known at the time their babies are born to the adoption agency or other qualified professionals that help place their children. Some of the birth couples I work with request regular communications with their adoptive families, usually

"Friends at school ask me if I'm Swedish because I am tall and have blond hair and blue eyes. I wish I knew the answer, but I don't. I don't know anything about my background. I don't remember being told I was adopted, but I think I figured it out when I was working on a project in grade school. For the project I needed to write about my heritage and background, and that got me started asking questions which led to a discussion about adoption with my parents."[13]—Allison, age 17

Ruth A. Mark has master's degrees in home economics (emphasis in parenting) and social work from Western Michigan University. She is a Licensed Clinical Social Worker and has been working in the adoption field since 1983. She is the Executive Director of Adoption Resource Services, Inc., with offices in Elkhart and Fort Wayne, Indiana. In this role, Mrs. Mark counsels birth couples throughout a pregnancy, hospital experience, adoptive placement, and as long as they desire thereafter. She also completes home studies and educates, prepares, and assesses prospective adoptive couples.

around birthdays and holidays, and others do not. We provide this communication through our agency to protect the confidentiality of all parties. Of course, sometimes birth couples move and forget to inform us about their new address and phone number. You could try contacting the attorney or other individuals your parents worked with when they placed you to see if they have your birth mother's wishes on file.

What if my parents get mad at me for trying to find my birth parents?

If your parents are uncomfortable with your search, it would be helpful for all of you to talk with a social worker or counselor. I spend a lot of time during the home study process working through emotions that adoptive couples might have about childlessness, infertility, a birth family's ongoing love for the child they place, and about the possibility that their child will want to search for their birth parents when he/she is older. If that type of counseling was not done with your parents, they may have some issues they will need to work through now with a counselor. You can discuss your concerns with your parents and also call an adoption social worker for assistance.

It's a Fact

According to a 2012 report by the Evan B. Donaldson Adoption Institute, 55 percent of infant adoptions are "open," 40 percent are "mediated," and only 5 percent are "closed."[14]

Another teen, Faith, age nineteen, finds she goes back and forth between wanting to meet her birth mother and deciding she should wait a little longer before starting her search. Faith is looking for information that she hopes will help resolve some of her fears and issues so she can move forward and search for her birth mother. Ms. Hollee McGinnis from the Evan B. Donaldson Adoption Institute responds to Faith's questions.

Some days I really want to search for my birth mother and other days I don't. One time I even called the adoption agency that placed me to begin the search process, but then I realized I was getting into something very big and got scared so I backed out. How do I know when I'm really ready to start my search?[15]

As adoptees we did not get to choose our adoptions. We did not choose to be relinquished. We did not choose to be adopted. The decision to search is one of the few things adoptees get to choose. It is a part of our adoption life journey; it is not our adoptive parents' journey. There is a right time for everybody. It is a very individual thing. I would recommend you listen to your gut, your heart, and have a clear mind. Do not listen to others who are enthusiastic about your search or

Hollee McGinnis is the Policy and Operations Director at the Evan B. Donaldson Adoption Institute in New York. Ms. McGinnis is also the editor for *TransCultured Magazine*. Ms. McGinnis was born in Korea and adopted by a family in the United States when she was three. In her twenties, she returned to Korea and met her birth parents and other members of her birth family. Recently, she was a part of a motherland tour to Korea and facilitated several reunions with adopted teens and their Korean birth families.

In 1996, Ms. McGinnis founded Also-Known-As, Inc. (AKA), an organization that recognizes and celebrates the community of people whose lives—through adoption—bridge nations, cultures, and races. AKA also started a Teen Mentorship Program in which international adolescent adoptees, ages 14–18, can explore their identity and race, build friendships with other internationally adopted teens, and be a part of a community in which international adolescent adoptees feel empowered and find their own voices. You can learn more about AKA on its website, www.akaworld.org.

reunion. Make sure the enthusiasm is yours. Do not feel pressured by your birth family or adoptive family to search or reunite until you are ready. Make sure that the choice is yours.

How do I get ready emotionally to find my birth mother? I don't want to have my hopes up too high. What should I be thinking before I meet her?

I have several thoughts you might want to consider as you prepare to meet your birth mother.

1. *Be willing to give up your expectations and childhood fantasies.* I think all adoptees create a fantasy about our birth parents whether we are conscious of it or not. As a child I would bounce between two extremes. On the one hand I thought I must be a princess and my birth parents were royalty. My older sister would tease me and say, "Yeah, you always were a princess—spoiled!" On the other hand I thought maybe my birth mom was a prostitute. I wondered, what if they did give me up because they did not want me? I simply did not know. What are your expectations, and what are your fantasies? Do you imagine that when you meet your birth family you will automatically connect, that you will find those real parents that you have been always been searching for? Are you willing to give up your expectations and childhood fantasies?

2. *Be ready to confront the knowledge about your past.* For many adoptees the years prior to our adoption are masked in mystery that we fill with our fantasies. I was not born a princess. My birth mother was a prostitute. She was also orphaned when she was nine years old, lived with an aunt until she was twelve, and survived by sheer will on the streets. She loved my birth father, who took her away from the brothel. They gave birth to me, and he promised to marry her but never did because Korean law forbade couples with the same last name to marry. I had to struggle with how this information fit into my life and defined who I was.

3. *Be prepared to not be in control.* I think those who have embarked on a search can attest to the roller coaster ride of emotions. You will not be in control. Currently there is no simple way of finding birth parents. Many agencies are not required by law to give adoptees information about their birth. There are ethical issues about birth parents' rights to confidentiality, which adoptees must respect. You may initiate the search, but most people find their birth parents through sheer luck and the kindness of strangers, not through careful planning.

4. *Be prepared to meet strangers.* I do not like to use the word "reunion" because for me, meeting my birth family was not a reunion. I did not remember

"The decision to search for one's birth parents is one of many milestones in our adoptions. Although we might try to create a road map based on another person's search, the reality is that when you were adopted, the age you were adopted or abandoned, what orphanage you were first placed at, what agency you were processed through, and the circumstances that led up to your relinquishment all affect your search and, ultimately, the outcome. Every search and reunion is unique."[16]—Hollee McGinnis, Policy and Operations Director, Evan B. Donaldson Adoption Institute

them. It was a "getting-to-know-you." People ask, "So, how was it? What was it like to meet your birth parents?" Sometimes it is good; sometimes it is bad. Sometimes it is very, very bad. Some adoptees search for years to find out that their birth parents do not want to meet them. Others realize that they are still the family secret. Even adoptees who remember their birth families realize how much they have changed since they were last with their birth families.

Teens Talk

Sasha, Age 19

"When I turned sixteen the search for my birth mother became almost 'instinctual.' She gave birth at sixteen and adopted through a closed adoption. I felt a strong connection with beginning my search at the age she had me. Little to my sixteen-year-old knowledge, though, did I know that you couldn't unlock the records until you were eighteen. At this I was frustrated, not being able to really understand why I couldn't search.

"Gaining and losing momentum I would randomly remind my mom sometimes that I was interested in searching, and although she gave me support as she always did, the searches always had holes. Frustrated by the law that sets the age for which I am able to search for my birth mother, I wait for my twenty-first birthday, and since the law in India has been changed, I'm wondering how long I'll never know. The search for my birth mother has been particularly relevant, for as a half-Asian half-black child, the search for identity has been particularly messy."[17]

Sasha

Getting Prepared

Before launching a search for your birth family, you need to be at peace with the fact that you have no control over if you will find them, or what they will be like when you find them. When you make the decision to start searching, that doesn't necessarily mean if you find them you have to embark on a long and close relationship, or spend every holiday together. Perhaps they will not become a major part of your life, but a healthy alternative might be to decide you will do your best to accept your birth family just as they are.

Strengthening existing relationships in your life before you go searching for your birth family will help prepare you for whatever you find. Knowing that you

It's a Fact

A major event in the life of an adopted person, such as the birth of a child or death of an adoptive parent, may trigger an adoptee to search for birth parents.[18]

"I think it is vital that you understand your motivations and why you want to meet your birth family before beginning a search. After receiving the letter from my paternal grandfather, I felt I had to meet them. I did not know why I wanted to meet them except for the fact they had contacted me. It was not until I was twenty-four that I understood my motivation for meeting my birth family: I wanted them to know I was all right. In the chaos of returning to Korea, meeting my birth family, and learning more about my past, I was able to hang onto this one truth."—Hollee McGinnis, Policy and Operations Director, Evan B. Donaldson Adoption Institute

have a group of family and friends who love you and support you will help you tremendously if you encounter some tough situations. For example, if you locate a member of your birth family but they do not wish to meet you, you will have the acceptance and love of others to fall back on.

Whether you end up searching or not and how much time you invest in a search is a personal matter. Be sure to give yourself as much time as you feel you need to make that crucial decision. Searching for members of your birth family is not a race. The faster you can locate them is not necessarily better.

Put Yourself in Their Shoes

As you think about the various reasons why you want or don't want to search, keep in mind that your birth parents may be going through a very similar process. They, too, are faced with the decision of whether or not to search for you. And if they do want to search, their options may be limited if they signed an agreement when you were placed stating they would not attempt to find you until you reach a certain age or ever. It's important that you do not base your decision of whether to look for a birth parent solely on the fact that they have not come looking for you. Maybe they have searched and couldn't find you. Maybe they can't search because of a legal agreement or other personal or health issues.

Adoptions, and the legal boundaries associated with them, can vary a great deal. The more you find out about your adoption and the agreements that were signed, the more you will know about your birth parents and how to search for them. One birth mother, Sheila, and her daughter were separated for years simply because a document called a waiver remained sealed in their adoption file. Much pain and frustration could have been avoided had either Sheila's daughter or her adoptive parents known that this waiver existed and that if they petitioned the court to unseal their adoption file they could have easily obtained it.

Sheila's Story

"When I was twenty years old I had an unplanned pregnancy. I decided, after intense deliberations and a lot of counseling, that adoption was the best plan for me and my baby. One of the many adoption papers I signed was one agreeing to the Pennsylvania law stating that I would *never* try to find my birth daughter. At the same time, I was offered the opportunity to sign a waiver that would allow my birth daughter to find me when she turned eighteen. I signed the waiver because I definitely wanted to have a relationship with her in the future, that is, if she wanted one too.

"Unfortunately, the adoption agency didn't give my birth daughter or her parents the information they needed to open the adoption file and check for the waiver. Sadly, my birth daughter spent a lot of time wondering why she'd been placed for adoption and why I didn't want to keep her. In my case, the waiver was there and she could have found all of the answers to her questions long before she actually did.

"I hoped that I would meet my birth daughter at some point in my life. Actually, I expected to meet her at some point. When her eighteenth birthday came and went, I decided that I might need to wait until later, perhaps after she started her own family. What I didn't know was that my birth daughter was doggedly determined to locate me, and she eventually succeeded. What a miracle! Her parents supported her search efforts and continue to be supportive of the relationship she has with me and my family, which includes my husband and three children, along with various aunts, uncles, cousins, and grandparents—all 'birth' of course."[19]

"My kids love knowing their birth families, and so do I. We are closer to the ones who cope with life well than the ones who don't. But that is true of our other relatives, too. As the adoptive mom, I think of my kids as having brought in-laws into our family just like I and my husband did. My kids tell me they think of their birth parents as the individuals they are. They are over being confused about them, mad at them for getting pregnant when they were not ready to raise a child, and scared of losing them yet again. Families absorb new members and grieve the loss of others."[20]

—Judy Stigger, adoptive mother and adoption professional

The lesson from this adoption story is simple—find out all you can about your own adoption. Ask questions. Seek the help of people who are well-educated in the adoption field such as an adoption support group or perhaps an adoption lawyer. Educate yourself about adoption procedures, laws, and your rights. Go back to the agency that placed you and inquire about your adoption. When it comes to the very personal decision of whether or not to search for your birth parents, make sure you weigh your desires, emotions, and facts that you know are true, not fears or ideas that you have created in your mind over the years.

What about You?

Every adoption and every adopted teen is different. You can ask the advice of many people about whether you should search, but in the end only you can make the final decision. If you decide to search, then start with the facts. Prepare as best you can so you have the best odds of succeeding, and go for it. Starting your search when *you* are ready is the key to success.

! It's a Fact

Most laws in the United States are based on British common law. But in the case of adoption, this is not true. The British based their first adoption laws, which were passed in 1926, on U.S. adoption laws. The state of Massachusetts passed the first significant adoption statute in the United States in 1851, titled "An Act to Provide for the Adoption of Children."[21]

Discussion Questions

Do you tend to think about your birth parents often, or not much at all?

Are any friends or family members encouraging you to search (or trying to stop you from searching) for your birth parents?

What fears do you have about searching for your birth parents?

Have you created any fantasies or dreams about what your birth parents might be like?

How do you think you feel if those fantasies or dreams weren't true?

Do you believe every adopted child should try to find his or her birth parents? Why?

Notes

1. Jonathan, e-mail correspondence, April 17, 2006.
2. Michael, e-mail correspondence, March 29, 2006.
3. Ulrich Muller and Barbara Perry, "Adopted Persons' Search for and Contact with Their Birth Parents I: Who Searches and Why?" *Adoption Quarterly* 4, no. 3 (2001): 5–37.
4. Coping.org, "Impact of Developmental Learning Disorders," www.coping.org/specialneeds/impac.htm#Confusion (accessed September 27, 2006).
5. Larry Silver, "Off to a Good Start," *Adoptive Families*, August 2006, 38.
6. Carol Barbieri, "Your Mother Would Know," *New York Times*, November 29, 2005.
7. Ruth Padawer, "Accord Would Open Records to Adoptees," *The Record*, January 23, 2007.
8. Graduate Students in the Counseling, Clinical, and School Psychology Program at the University of California, Santa Barbara, "Attention Deficit Hyperactivity Disorder," www.education.ucsb.edu/jimerson/adhd.html (accessed September 28, 2006).
9. Mark Lerner, "Psychologist: ADHD and Adopted Children," international.adoption.com/foreign/psychologist-adhd-and-adopted-children.html (accessed September 28, 2006).
10. Ulrich Muller and Barbara Perry, "Adopted Persons' Search for and Contact with Their Birth Parents II: Adoptee–Birth Parent Contact." *Adoption Quarterly* 4, no. 3 (2001): 39–62.
11. Lisa, author interview, September 10, 2006.
12. Lisa, author interview, September 6, 2006.
13. Allison, author interview, August 26, 2006.
14. Evan B. Donaldson Institute, "Openness in Adoption: From Secrecy and Stigma to Knowledge and Connections," March 2012, www.adoptioninstitute.org/research/2012_03_openness.php (accessed March 28, 2012).
15. Faith, author interview, April 17, 2006.
16. Hollee McGinnis, e-mail correspondence, December 5, 2006.
17. Sasha, e-mail correspondence, March 4, 2006.
18. American Adoption Congress, "Frequently Asked Questions," www.americanadoptioncongress.org/faqs.htm (accessed April 13, 2005).
19. Sheila, e-mail correspondence, June 22, 2006.
20. Judy Stigger, e-mail correspondence, May 16, 2006.
21. Christine Adamec and William L. Pierce, *The Encyclopedia of Adoption* (New York: Facts on File, Inc., 2000), xviii.

SEARCHING FOR BIRTH PARENTS

"When I was twenty-one I decided I was ready to meet my birth mother. My parents went to court and opened my adoption records. With that information it didn't take long to find my birth mother. At first I wrote her a letter, then we talked on the phone, and eventually we met.

"Finding my birth father has been very difficult. After eleven years of asking questions and chasing clues, I still find myself grasping at straws and winding up at dead ends. My birth mother will not help me in my search—she won't even tell me his first name. I'm not giving up though. Someday I hope I will stumble across the right piece of information that will lead me to my birth father."[1]—Sarah, age 32

Have you longed to find your birth parents ever since you first learned you were adopted? Did a certain event in your life create a sudden urgent need to find them? Or has your decision to find your birth parents been a long process, with new feelings and emotions slowly unfolding over time that eventually resulted in a desire to find them? Throughout the course of history, thousands of adoptees have reached the same conclusion—they want to meet their biological parents. Some took a few weeks or months to arrive at their decision, while others spent years or even decades to make up their minds. In the end, it is a choice that should be made thoughtfully and carefully, no matter how long it takes.

Once you have made this momentous decision, finding your birth parents may be easy or it may be very difficult. For some teens, finding a birth parent may be as simple as picking up the phone and calling the adoption agency that handled their placement to obtain contact information. Perhaps your parents have been holding information about your birth parents, waiting until they thought you were old enough or mature enough to know what you wanted to do with it. For other adopted teens, the path that leads to a birth parent can be long and confusing. And after many tiresome miles down a rocky road, you may discover that you

A Time to Celebrate

Every year the president of the United States officially proclaims November as National Adoption Month. People throughout the United States celebrate adoption and honor adoptive families for this entire month. The history of National Adoption Month can be traced back to 1976, when the governor of Massachusetts first proclaimed Adoption Week. In 1988, President Ronald Reagan made Adoption Week an official national event. National Adoption Week became National Adoption Month in 1990.[2]

National Adoption Day is celebrated on the Saturday before Thanksgiving every year. Hundreds of events are held throughout the country on National Adoption Day. You can visit www.nationaladoptionday.org for ideas about ways you can celebrate. Why not plan to do something special with your family on that day?

were on the wrong road all along! If information about your birth parents is not easy to find, don't give up. With a little investigative work, some patience, and a lot of persistence, you may be able to navigate the unknown path ahead and find your birth parents.

Getting Your Parents on Board

Most likely, your parents are the ones who can help you the most in your search for your birth parents. If your parents are worried or hesitant about this prospective meeting, it will probably be much more difficult for you to gather critical information about your adoption. To help alleviate your parents' fears, and hopefully get them on board with your desire to find your birth parents, it's best to discuss everyone's feelings and get them out in the open. By sharing your thoughts, you can help your parents see your point of view. Let your parents know that you appreciate all they have done for you, and that you love and care for them. Although they are adults, they may need to be reassured that your feelings for them will not change if you find your birth parents. Be honest and share with them why this search is important to you. If your parents are struggling with your decision to meet your birth parents, you might find your first task is to convince them that meeting your birth parents is a good idea before you start your search. This next section will hopefully give you some tools to help your parents understand your needs and, eventually, support your decision to search.

Timing Is Everything

Explaining to your parents why you want to search may require a little planning. First off, remember that timing is crucial. Carefully choose the best time to make your request. The middle of a fight is probably not a great time to say, "And by the way, I want to search for my birth mom, and you can't stop me!" Think about how your parents like to be approached. For instance, if dinnertime is when your family usually talks about family business, try that. If you want to have a conversation without your siblings present, you might ask a parent for a ride somewhere or use a shopping trip as an opportunity to talk. If your parents don't like surprises, let them know early in the day that you have something important to talk about at dinner.

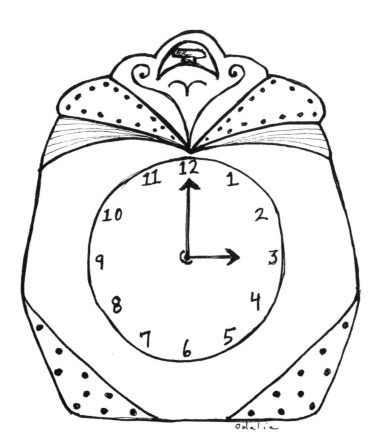

It's All in the Delivery

Have you ever noticed how some comedians know exactly how to say a joke so that the entire audience ends up rolling in laughter? Have you ever told the same joke to your friends and they didn't even smile? The difference is that a comedian knows how to set up a joke—give the audience the right bits of information in a certain order and at just the right pace. Comedians spend hours practicing their "delivery," and that's a skill you can use when you tell your parents about your desire to find your birth parents, or any other potentially shocking news.

When you want to make a good delivery, you need to think about what approach has worked in the past when discussing a difficult topic with your parents. In some families, the direct approach works well. Some parents like to hear their teen simply and directly say what he or she is thinking or wants. Other parents may need time to digest an idea before they are ready to discuss it with you.

If your parents like to think about things before they are ready to give an opinion, try writing your mom or dad a letter or an e-mail. Put a note in a card on their dresser to introduce the topic. This method gives your parents time to process the idea of searching for your birth parents before you sit down and talk together. Another tactic is to ask someone else, like an uncle or older sibling, to bring up the topic. You might know that your parents would respond more calmly to someone they respect or have confidence in. Perhaps the conversation would go smoother if another trusted person were present when you make your request, such as a counselor, pastor, or a grandparent. You should brief that person ahead of time on what you plan to say. This third party might have ideas on how to present your search request in a manner more likely to fly with your parents.

Use the Right Script

Sometimes difficult conversations go best if they are planned, or scripted, ahead of time. Here are five main elements to include in your discussion as you try to convince your parents to help you search for your birth parents: *reassure, explain, request, prepare, reassure again*. As you begin your talk with your parents, remember—if they become upset during your discussion and don't allow you to talk, calmly ask them to hear you out.

Reassurance Paves the Way

If you think your parents are worried that you are looking for "new and improved" parents, then reassuring them up front may get rid of those fears that

> **! It's a Fact**
>
> In a 2002 national survey sponsored by the Dave Thomas Foundation for Adoption, 82 percent of the respondents stated that if they were thinking about adopting, a major concern they would have is to make sure the birth parents could not take the child back after placement.[3] Of course, once an adoption is final, the birth parents have no parental rights, and it is virtually impossible for them to take the child back.

could block your conversation. You might try saying something like, "Before I ask for your help on something, I want you to know that you are and will always be my real parents."

Your parents may also fear that after your birth parents meet you, they will try to "horn in" on your family. Deep down your parents may be scared that these new intruders will try to take over as your parents or even want to take you back permanently. In very personal matters, even logical and seemingly rational parents can imagine some irrational scenarios. Chances are, with a little reassurance, even reluctant parents will eventually come around and want to help.

Explain Your Reasons

You have given a good deal of thought to searching for your birth parents, but remember, your parents may be caught off guard by your sudden request. Sharing some of your thought process may help them see that finding your birth parents is important to you. As you share your reasons, they may discover some valid points that will convince them to help. Although there are numerous reasons that adopted teens have for wanting to find their birth parents, five of the most common ones, which are also explained in more detail in chapter 5, are listed below. Reviewing this information may help you present your own reasons clearly to your parents.

1. Genetics

Often, adopted children in their teen years start to have questions about their abilities or struggles. Maybe you wonder why you are good in math, tend to be hyper, have great coordination, or can't spell no matter how hard you study. Perhaps you dream of playing in the NBA and just want to know how tall your biological parents are. Something as seemingly insignificant as a genetics lesson in a biology class can spark an interest in learning about your biological parents. If your parents are interested in family history or researching their heritage, they might respond to this type of reasoning.

2. Medical History

Sometimes teens develop a health problem that leads them to wonder about their medical history. As everyone knows, parents are very concerned with the health of their children and will logically see the value of this rationale. Even if you have some medical information about your birth parents, you may find that seventeen years later you would like an update. Knowing health information about your birth mother and birth father (and their extended families) can be invaluable in diagnosing and preventing health problems.

3. Improving Your Self-Esteem

Self-esteem is something that you may not fully understand or may be difficult to talk about with others. Even though you may feel accepted and loved by your parents, there may be some unexplainable void you are also feeling. Self-esteem is how you feel about yourself, whether positive or negative. Some adopted teens express a need to find their birth parents to feel more complete, or better, about themselves.

4. Concern for Your Birth Mother

Some teens are very happy with their adoptive family yet find they are worried about their birth mother. They want to reassure her that she made a good decision when she made an adoption plan. This type of strong concern for others is called altruism. Most parents would probably be very pleased to learn that they have raised such a caring child. If you feel the need to comfort your birth mother, or think that knowing she is okay would be a great comfort to you, share this with your parents.

5. Future Planning

The teen years are often spent planning for the future. Perhaps you are beginning to think about and plan for college. You may be spending a great deal of time thinking about various jobs and how to prepare for them. Many teens want to know what other people in their birth family are good at and what kind of work they do. Your birth family may not have had the educational opportunities you do, but knowing their aptitudes and skills may give you some clues as you make educational and job choices.

Make Your Request

Once you've shared your reasons for wanting to find your birth parents, you may need to give your parents time to digest your ideas. When you feel the time is right, state your request simply: "Would you help me look for my birth mother or father?"

Show That You're Prepared

Showing your parents that you are prepared will definitely make them feel better about this whole process. If you made a list of the best- and worst-case scenarios that might happen as you search (see chapter 5), you should discuss this list with your parents. The things you have listed under the "worst" column are probably what your parents are most concerned about and perhaps the reason they are reluctant to help you with your search. They want to protect you from being hurt. Demonstrate that you are aware of the possibility of being hurt and appreciate the love that comes with their worry. Ask them to add to your list. Sometimes parents know about or suspect there is something difficult in your history. If you can cover that "something," your parents are more likely to decide you are able to handle a search.

End with More Reassurance

As you end your script about why you want to search for your birth parents, you need to realize that you have given your parents a lot to think about. The thought of you meeting your birth parents may cause them a great deal of stress. And the more stress they feel, the more they are not likely to think clearly and respond in a negative way. You can lower their stress by reassuring them again that they are and always will be your parents. Close your presentation by saying something like, "I think that if we work together on this, it will bring us closer. I really hope you will decide to help me find my birth parents."

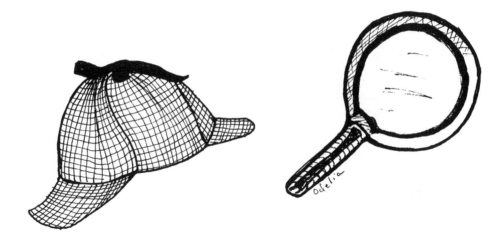

Becoming a Detective

Now that you've hopefully enlisted the help of your parents, you are ready to play detective. First, get a notebook to keep all the information you gather in one place. You will need to keep your clues organized and together. Sometimes one small piece of information can lead you down the right path to finding your birth parents. Of course, your adoptive parents are the best people to interview and start gathering facts from.

Here are some questions to ask as you start your search:

- Where was I born (city, state, country)?
- What is the name of the hospital where I was born?
- How old was I when I was adopted?
- Was I placed through an agency? If so, what is its address and phone number?
- What other people were involved in my adoption (social workers, lawyers, judges, etc.)?
- What information is known about my birth parents?
- Are there any letters or photos from my birth parents?

Try asking family members such as grandparents, aunts, uncles, older siblings, or even past babysitters for stories they remember about your adoption. You may uncover a family story or even a bit of gossip that will prove helpful. If you don't mind others knowing your business, neighbors where you lived when you were a small child might recall some useful information too. As you gather information, try not to get distracted by chasing after a small lead. Just focus on

In the 1930s many states passed laws that required the birth certificates of adopted children to be sealed. (When a birth certificate is sealed, it is not available for anyone to obtain or read.) It was thought that sealing this private information would protect the privacy of the birth mother, the adopted child, and the adoptive parents from meddling outsiders. Lawmakers also wanted to make sure that adoptive families completely assumed all responsibilities for their adopted child. The practice of sealing adoption records made it very difficult, if not impossible in some cases, for a birth mother and adopted child to find one another in later years.[4]

collecting all the facts you can, and then sit down later and decide which pieces of information are worth pursuing.

As you collect answers to your questions, be sure to write down every detail. Even the smallest of clues can lead to a breakthrough in your search. Also, ask to see your birth certificate and make a copy to keep in your notebook. Your birth certificate will most likely be an amended copy, meaning your adoptive parents will be listed on the certificate as your parents and your birth parents will not be mentioned at all. But it will have your correct birth date and other helpful information such as the name of the hospital where you were born and the delivery doctor's name.

Teens Ask

Three teens, Allison, Andrew, and Faith, have some questions about searching for their birth parents. Adoption professional Judy Stigger provides a wealth of helpful information in her answers that follow.

It's a Fact

Ideas about adoption and adoption records began to change in the 1970s. In recent years, adoption advocates have pushed for more open adoptions and the opening of adoption records.

Judy Stigger, LCSW, is a social worker with over twenty years' experience working with adoptive families and adopted children/teens. She is a published author, helped start www.AdoptionLearningPartners.org, and has served on boards for *Adoptive Families* magazine, JCICS (the organization of international adoption agencies), and for a group of internationally adopted young adults finding their voice in society. Ms. Stigger is the adoptive mom of two children, transracially placed and now grown. She and her children searched when her children were in grade school and they both asked for contact with their birth families. Each birth mother and, years later, one birth father was found, and they keep in touch.

When can I start to look for my birth parents? Is there a certain age?[25]—Allison, age 17

The quick answer is: you can start looking at any age. The time to start depends on whose help you need to search and what you hope happens if you succeed in finding a birth relative.

Many people mistakenly assume that you have to be eighteen or twenty-one before you can start to search. In fact, people can and routinely do search much earlier than that. But if you seek help from a state government service, such as an Adoption Search Registry, or the agency or whoever helped arrange your adoption, laws in your state may dictate that a teen needs parental permission to receive information. In some states, certain information cannot be released even with parental permission until you are an adult. Each state enacts its own laws and procedures for foster care, adoption, and searches. Every state is different. Agencies must follow the laws applicable to them, even if they would like to help you more than the law allows. To move forward, assess what information you already have, determine what help you need, secure parental cooperation if possible, and then sort out how much assistance you will be able to secure through official channels and how much you are going to have to figure out on your own. Some searches only require a few weeks. Others last a lifetime.

How do I tell my parents I want to search without hurting their feelings?[26]—Faith, age 19

You are more likely to find your birth parents and have a pleasant experience meeting if you have parental cooperation. You are probably going to need information about your early background to help you begin a successful search. A parent often has such records. Access to Agency or State Registry information requires parental consent for a teen. And parental emotional support can help you through the dead ends and tough decisions.

Some teens have adoptive parents who are helpful about searching, but not so gung ho that they take over the search and make it their own. If you are one of those lucky teens, remember to thank your parents for being supportive. As a teen, it may be helpful to consider why your parents might be nervous about your search.

When adopted teens tell their parents they wish to start searching for their birth family, some parents may worry that their teen is looking for a nicer or younger mom or dad. Others may be concerned that their child will feel loyalty to their birth family and pull away from the adoptive family emotionally. Another common concern adoptive parents have is that their child will learn painful information about why placement happened or how the birth family are now faring, and be hurt by that information. Perhaps their adopted teen may even want to rescue the birth family. Another fear is that their child won't be able to find any birth family or will be rejected by them and be hurt by the experience.

Parents worried about such scenarios may not provide the cooperation you need. It might help you understand your parents' possible concerns if you discover a little bit more about their situation. For example, if your parents were unable to give birth because they were infertile, they may now hold this strong desire to be able to offer you everything you need. Birth parents can provide information that your adoptive parent cannot, and this reminds your adoptive parents that they don't hold your genetic information; some other parent does. Your parents may feel threatened or saddened by this fact.

The reassurance parents often need is that you and they are always and forever a family, although you are not a "biological" one. You are not looking for better or different parents. You are just looking for missing information about your background and what it might imply for your future.

Parents may also worry that the birth family might want the teen to get really involved in the birth family and that the teen will be torn between loyalties and not be sure how to cope with the demands of two family systems. The reassurance a parent may crave is that you know who your family is and will be thoughtful about how involved or invested you become in your birth family. You can invite your parents to keep you company in becoming acquainted with your birth family.

Some parents might be concerned that what you find in your search may be something unpleasant: that you are the result of a date rape, or that you were an embarrassment to your birth grandparents, or that your birth mom tried to abort you. They worry that you will find a birth mom whose life is a mess because of a condition such as addiction or extreme poverty. Acknowledge to your parents that such information would be tough to learn. Just knowing that your birth mom made an adoption plan for you is tough for many teens.

"Often the focus on a search is on the quest, but the true journey begins after you meet your birth family and are left with the question, 'Now what?' Are you going to continue this relationship? Or are you satisfied with the reunion and do not wish to have further contact? If your birth parents are poor, do you feel an obligation to help them? Will you try to travel to Korea once a year? Will you send gifts for the holidays and remember birthdays? You have traded in your fantasies, your dreams, and imaginations for reality, and after the reunion you will not be able to simply tuck these people back into the farthest corners of your mind. You have seen their faces; you know who they are; you have seen their lives. Meeting your birth family may answer some questions but raise far more questions. The search is only the beginning of the journey. Life after the reunion will be a far longer road."[7]—Hollee McGinnis, Policy and Operations Director, Evan B. Donaldson Adoption Institute

If your parents have not had any contact with your birth family over the years, they may fear that if you search and can't find or are rejected by a birth family member, you may be deeply hurt or feel as if you have no value. In reality, any of these things could happen. Your job is to prepare yourself and make sure you have thought about the worst-case scenarios carefully before you start your search. You might tell your parents that you think you can manage such situations—with their help.

How do I get started looking for my birth mom?[8]—Andrew, age 17

You can start your quest by focusing on three areas:

- Collecting and reviewing available background information
- Exploring options for assistance available to you by your state's laws
- Preparing yourself, so you can respond quickly if opportunity arises

Background

First, gather all available documents and pieces of information related to your adoption. Usually your parents are the easiest source. They may have more infor-

"Sometimes when I go to crowded places, like the mall, I search for my birth parents. I look for women who I think would be about the right age and study their faces to see if they look like me. I know that seems crazy, but for some reason I think I might find my birth parents. Other adopted friends have admitted they do the same thing."[9]—Laura, age 18

mation than they realize. Read birth certificates, court documents related to your foster care or adoption, medical records, agency summaries, anything. If you are referred to as "Baby Boy Johnson," then one of your birth parents' last names is probably Johnson. If you are lucky, the name is not Johnson but something less common. Where were you born? Might that be the town your birth grandparent still lives in? If an open adoption agency or search group exists in your area, call (or ask your parent to call) and inquire if someone there would review your documents with you. Folks who have searched before will know what to look for as well as the rules for getting information in your state. (There are "adoption search and reunion groups" on Google Groups in many states and Canada. Or go on www.Adoption.com, click "reunions," and read lots of stories and good ideas.)

Warning: Please, don't go on the Internet and talk about how you are looking for your birth parents. Creepy older guys, who go looking for teens to mess with, will sometimes pose as a birth father who would welcome meeting you. Such men have tricked teens before, and they become skilled at taking advantage. Several teens I have worked with were contacted by predators and were initially convinced they had found their birth dads. One individual posed as a teen's birth brother. He said that he had been looking for her and was so excited that he might have found the birth sister he had learned about from their mom. He had great lines about how their birth mom had told him about her. He had done his homework and knew a lot about her. The police had to get involved to ward off the guy, who turned out to be in his 40s and a known pedophile. This teen was smart and cautious, but our lives are pretty public these days. Anyone who reads your school site, your My Space or Facebook profile, or that of other teens your age from your school and their replies to each other may learn a lot about you and sound like they know stuff only your birth family could know.

One other caution: Don't click on the paid ads for private search listings and services. Some are fine, but some will just invade your privacy or try to talk you out of money. Your state's adoption registry, if it has one, is a much better place to list yourself. If you were born in another state, you might consider registering in that state as well. Ask your parents to support you with their permission. (I know this is tough advice if your parents are not going to be helpful. But it's better for you to be safe and wait to search in several years when you are an adult than to get hurt or have a fearful experience now.)

Do not be surprised if you decide you want to take a break after reading your background information. Some people find looking at their early life history, in the stark black-and-white of documents, emotionally sufficient for the time being. If you decide to take a break, be assured that you can resume your search when it feels right to you to do so. If your parents are eager to help you search, you can explain that many people who start a search take breaks at various points in the process—sometimes for years. You are totally normal in the decisions you are making.

Exploring Assistance Options

While you are reviewing documents, your parents can explore whether other information is available. As your guardian, they can ask for your complete hospital records, assuming the hospital still exists. They might try asking under your birth name. The hospital may cooperate. Sometimes you learn a great deal about your birth and birth family.

The agency or lawyer or whoever helped arrange your adoption may be willing to give information. They may know the name of the birth family. They may or may not be able to share that with you, depending on the laws of your state and what promises they made to that birth family fifteen or so years ago. Even if they cannot share birth family confidential information with you, they may be able to contact the birth family on your behalf to ask if the birth family is willing to be contacted by you. We found the birth mother of one of my kids in a month because the agency we used was willing to try contacting the birth family—and luckily the family had not moved.

In some states your parents can sign up on the adoption search or reunion registry on your behalf. To find the registry for a particular state, try a Google search such as "adoption reunion registry" followed by the initials for the state in which you were born or the state in which your birth family might think you are currently living. Call a local adoption agency listed on the web or in the phone book as supporting open adoption. Usually agencies that support open adoption will also support an adoptive person's desire to search. Try www.adoption.com and click on the "reunions" tab to find some lists of the state registries along with thought-provoking articles.

Some agencies and/or search groups may be able to suggest a private investigator whom they have used and found trustworthy. If someone mentions a name to you, discuss this option and the expenses with your parents.

One of the largest adoption registries is the International Soundex Reunion Registry, which was founded in 1975. This nonprofit registry is free and open to adopted adults over eighteen, birth parents, and adoptive parents of children under eighteen years of age. It is a "mutual consent" registry, which means both the adopted child and birth parent must register on the site. If a match is found, then the adopted child and birth parent will be notified. You can check out the ISRR website at www.isrr.org.[10]

Prepare Yourself

In searching for a birth parent, you may sometimes find you must act quickly or lose an opportunity. It's best to prepare yourself beforehand so you are able to make the most of a sudden opportunity.

For example, let's say that you were adopted through the agency for which I work. You go online, download the required forms from the postadoption section of the agency website, and ask us to contact your birth family. After the paperwork and some conversation, we ask you to write a note and include a picture that can be sent to your birth family. We ask for materials because if we find a birth family member, they will be much more excited to hear from you than from an agency. If we find them, we can offer to forward a note from you, which can include your contact information if you wish. In this situation, you need to be ready. Writing a letter to your birth family, before you even know if anyone can find them, is tough. But if you can make yourself do a first draft, you'll start yourself thinking. Birth moms often worry that you will judge them harshly for getting pregnant when they were not ready to raise you and for giving you up for adoption. You might want to mention that you are not mad at her, but rather curious to learn more about her. Add that you appreciate her making an adoption plan to care for you, even though you think that was painful for her to do. You can also ask a parent if they would be willing to write a little note so that your birth family knows that your family is okay with this search and is looking forward to meeting, too. That will start your mom or dad thinking.

Another thing to consider before you find your birth parents is whether you want long-term contact. In order to think about that now, try picturing the type of birth parent you think you would want to stay in touch with. You don't actually know them yet, so this may be hard. This exercise is important because I have seen people rush into getting to know each other so intensely that soon one party feels overwhelmed and backs away. Then expectations get thwarted and feelings get hurt. Since you are initiating this possible relationship, you owe it to yourself, your family, and your birth family to begin giving the long-range possibilities some thought.

Various reunion groups have members who will share their stories about finding a birth parent with your family, or a counselor from an open adoption agency may be willing to meet with you and your parents for an hour and help you think about the possibilities. This is probably worth your time.

Once I know where my birth parents are, what do I do?—Andrew, age 17

If you contact your birth mother in a disconcerting way, she might back away. If you contact her gently, you improve the odds that she will respond to your overture. Think about starting with a letter to her. Tell her why you think she might be your birth mother. Write a little about who you've grown up to be. What are your skills, hobbies, and school activities? Talk about why you want to meet her, what you hope to learn, and that you are not asking to intrude or for money. Share with her what you hope she will do in response to this letter. For example, "I hope you will e-mail me or write me back soon. I want to know if you are okay with me contacting you like this. Just so you know, my parents are supportive of my getting acquainted with you and would enjoy meeting you someday too." Ask a few questions that she can answer back. Nothing heavy like, "Why didn't you keep me?" Light questions such as "What do you like to do for fun?" would be a great way to start out.

Some adoptive persons or birth parents want to meet as soon as they find each other. One adopted teen described his meeting as "the most important blind date of my life." Others develop a relationship gently and over time, getting to know a little about each other before meeting face-to-face. E-mail is a great vehicle for getting to know each other a step at a time.

You probably want to talk to your parents about how you would handle a first meeting. What follows are suggestions for meeting, whether you meet immediately or have corresponded for a long time before you meet. If you e-mail or talk on the phone before you meet, the strongest suggestion I have is that you talk about how you want that first meeting to go and then discuss plans with your parents. Everyone is so nervous that you can start by talking about how scared and excited you are to meet, and that should initiate a conversation. Ask your parents for their suggestions too. And ask one of them to be your support person, if they won't make you more nervous by being there.

What do most birth moms say when you find them?—Allison, age 17

Remember, you have been searching, and thinking about searching for a while. Your birth mother doesn't know you have been searching and will quite possibly be surprised to hear from you. Just as you are in a different situation in life than you were twelve or sixteen years ago, so is she. She may be married. She may have children who do not know about you. You may find your birth grandmother first, because that is who still lives at the last known address. She may or may not know about you. Or you find a birth sibling who was also adopted; and his or her adoptive family is about to be surprised by your contact. The range of possibilities is endless.

You can't plan for every contingency. You can think about how to be gentle and discreet as you first approach a possible birth family member. Since this issue is really emotional, you may want someone else to make the first contact, especially if it is going to be a live phone call.

Predicting the response to your first contact is impossible. People vary. There are three basic reactions you might get—happy, indifferent, or negative—and all sorts of variations in between.

As an adopted teen, you hope your birth parent will be thrilled to hear from you—and in many reunions, this is the case. Every adopted person who goes searching hopes to hear this response from a birth parent: "I've been waiting to see you since the day I placed you."

Some birth parents may react with some indifference. You might hear something like, "I'm glad to hear that my birth son (or daughter) is okay, but I'm not sure if I want to talk to him (or her) or meet. I've never told my husband about that baby. And I can't imagine how I would tell my kids that I had a baby I gave up for adoption before I had them." This ambivalent birth mother may not respond now but may be ready for more contact in a year or two.

A negative reaction from a birth parent can be very hard to take, but remember that there may be immediate circumstances causing this type of response. Perhaps after further discussion a birth mother might share, "I'm going through a divorce right now. The last thing I need is for a child to show up making my life more complicated." As you conduct your search, ask yourself these questions: Will I feel okay about myself if my birth family responds poorly in my search? If my search doesn't go well, how will I handle my feelings of anger, frustration, or sadness? If you don't feel you have adequate answers now, perhaps you should stop searching until you do.

What if I can't find my birth mother?—Allison, age 17

How frustrating! This happens—both locally and internationally. Sometimes you have so little information to work with, or what you were told is wrong, or the agency that did your adoption had a flood and the records were destroyed.

For some, the knowledge that they searched brings some degree of closure. For others, the missing information leaves an emotional hole in their heart that

MIA–Missing Information: All

Some adopted teens do not have any information about their birth family. This situation occurs in some international adoptions where a child is placed from an agency that was not required to collect background information about birth parents. Some are not able to obtain information because the child was abandoned and the agency did not have any contact with the birth parents. Sometimes birth parents are ashamed or afraid to place a child, so they opt to anonymously leave their baby somewhere they feel is safe, like the steps of an adoption agency, police station, or church.

Several U.S. states provide places called "safe havens" where a mother can leave her baby and know the child will be properly cared for. While this service provides birth mothers with an easy and safe place to take a child they cannot care for, it also results in some children who are placed for adoption and later find they have no records about their past. Workers at designated safe havens—a hospital, police station, or manned fire station—are instructed to ask the birth parents several questions to obtain some background information. The laws regarding safe havens vary in each state. For example, the Safe Haven Act of Massachusetts (2004) states that a birth parent may leave a newborn seven days old or younger at properly designated facilities if there is no sign of child abuse or neglect. Most states will take babies up to around three weeks old, while some will accept a child that is a few months old.[11]

If you discover your birth parents are "missing in action," this can be a terrible blow. Not only because you are not able to meet and get to know them, but also because you cannot get answers to some of the questions you've had for years—questions about your birth mother's situation and her reasons for placing you, medical information, or if you have half brothers or sisters. If you find yourself unable to find any new information about your birth parents and your search seems impossible, there may come a time when you need to stop searching and move on with your life. It may help you work through your disappointment by focusing your energy on your adoptive family and strengthening those relationships. Spend some time thinking about what they have given you in the past, such as unconditional love, great memories, support, and encouragement.

will always be there. How do you live and love well with a hole in your heart? Also, the lack of background information, especially medical, can be a real inconvenience if you have health issues.

I have two ideas which may or may not give you comfort. First, with the expansion of the Internet and the availability of DNA testing to establish biological parent connections, some adopted people hold out hope for the future. They believe that new advances in technology may help them find their birth parents in later years.

> "I see lots of doctors because of medical problems. I get so tired of filling out the family history section with 'I don't know' over and over again."[12]
> —Jen, age 18

Second, just because your birth parents can't be found does not mean that they have forgotten you or that you have to forget about them. If you don't have a memory of them, do things that honor your image of them. Light a candle for them on your birthday. Buy a big plastic storage container and put your thoughts, writings, or things that you would like to have shared with them into it. If you are religious, say a prayer on Father's Day and Mother's Day that they are well. You can also respect your birth parents by not making them all bad by thinking, "she didn't care about me anyway," or all good, by accepting the mantra "she'd probably let me do stuff my mom doesn't allow." Your birth mom is neither your fairy godmother nor a wicked stepmom. She is a person who became pregnant when she could not care for you in the way she wanted or needed to, and then made the best choice she could for you given her understanding of what was right and what options she had. How wise or stupid her decisions were do not reflect your worth (or your worth to her), but on what she was able to do—both for herself and for you.

Because your feelings about being adopted/abandoned originate from when you were very young, wrapping a mature understanding around your early adoption feelings is hard. A counselor who specializes in serving adopted persons and adoptive families may be able to help—not because you are crazy or need fixing, but because the counselor has heard from many other adopted persons who have had similar thoughts about this stuff. She can share those thoughts with you and save you having to figure it out by yourself. My mom used to say, "Don't reinvent the wheel." This goes for living with adoption too.

> "You may discover that in the process of searching for a birth parent, you learn more about yourself, your values, your ideals, and your dreams."[13]
> —Barbara Hayes, LCSW, ACSW

What about You?

How you go about searching for your birth family depends on what information and assistance is available to you. Whether you succeed in finding your birth family hinges on your effort, persistence, the records that are available to you, and many factors out of your control. Some say it depends even more on luck, fate, or God's will. If you are unable to find your birth family, take comfort in knowing you did your best. You made the search and that took courage. Enjoy the adoptive family you have been given. Who knows, perhaps the future still holds the reunion you long for.

A "successful" search is not necessarily one that ends with you meeting your birth parents. A success for you may mean discovering a piece of information about your past or birth family that answers an important question, which will allow you to move forward in your life. Maybe it means you found a picture of your birth mother and you learned that you have her eyes. If you do find and meet members of your birth family, acknowledge them for who they are—people who made the best decisions they could despite their flaws. People who love you and express that love in their own way. People who are a part of the unique and special group of people you call "family."

Discussion Questions

Have you ever discussed searching for your birth parents with your parents?

What information do you have about your birth parents?

Have you ever tried to search for your birth parents?

Are you prepared to start a search that may end up taking several months or even years?

What would you do if you couldn't find either of your birth parents?

Notes

1. Sarah, e-mail correspondence, July 29, 2006.
2. Adoption Clubhouse, "History of Adoption," www.adoptionclubhouse.org/03_homework/02_history/06_today.html (accessed February 27, 2006).
3. The Evan B. Donaldson Institute, "2002 National Adoption Attitudes Survey Highlights," www.adoptioninstitute.org/survey/survey_summary.html (accessed August 7, 2006).
4. Christine Adamec and William L. Pierce, *The Encyclopedia of Adoption* (New York: Facts on File, Inc., 2000), xviii.

5. Allison, author interview, August 26, 2006.
6. Faith, author interview, April 17, 2006.
7. Hollee McGinnis, e-mail correspondence, December 5, 2006.
8. Andrew, e-mail correspondence, March 17, 2006.
9. Laura (name changed), personal interview, September 6, 2006.
10. International Soundex Reunion Registry, www.isrr.net (accessed February 27, 2006).
11. Baby Safe Haven, www.babysafehaven.com/index.htm (accessed September 26, 2006).
12. Jen (name changed), author interview, March 12, 2006.
13. Barbara Hayes, e-mail correspondence, May 23, 2006.

MEETING BIRTH PARENTS

"If I wrote a letter to my birth mother, I would just invite her to hang out sometime. I would love to meet and hear about her life. I think it would be a pretty awesome conversation. I'd also like to know if my biological father died of heart disease at thirty or was schizophrenic—I would definitely want a heads up on something like that. In many ways, meeting her would just be like any other person I've met over a cigarette waiting for a train, except for the fact that I was in her uterus as a fetus at one point."[1]—Billy, age 19

Billy

You've made the decision to meet your birth parent or birth parents. You've found your contact information. You've explained why you must take this journey to your adoptive parents in the best way you know how. Perhaps they support this meeting, perhaps they don't. Maybe you don't fully understand their feelings, but you do know you must meet your birth parents before moving on in your life. You hope for the best and try not to think about the worst. But deep down inside, you know you must go through with your plan to meet your birth parents.

So now what? How can you prepare yourself emotionally for the biggest meeting in your life? The following Teens Ask section provides answers

Movie Marquee

Many adoptive teens feel as if their life is like a movie and they arrived at the theater after it already started. Even though they are enjoying the story, most would like to know what they missed at the beginning.

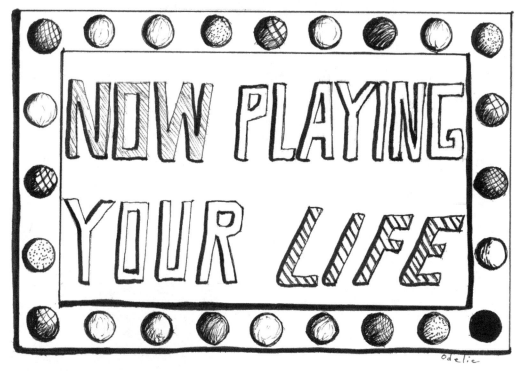

to some of the most common concerns adopted teens face when they prepare to meet their birth parents.

Teens Ask

Andrew, a seventeen-year-old adopted teen, asks several questions on the topic of meeting birth parents.[2] His questions are answered by Barbara Hayes, LCSW, ACSW.

I have always wanted to meet my birth parents, but I'm worried that it would be quite awkward. How should I prepare myself for this meeting?

Barbara Hayes is a Licensed Clinical Social Worker, a member of the Academy of Certified Social Workers, and has many years of experience working with both birth mothers and adoptive families. Ms. Hayes is the former Director of Birthright in Houston, Texas, and Richmond, Indiana. After receiving her MSW from Indiana University Graduate School of Social Work, Ms. Hayes worked for Metropolitan Family Services in Wheaton, Illinois, in both Clinical Counseling and the Post-Adoption Program. In 2007, Ms. Hayes was in private practice in Illinois. She is married and the adoptive mother of three children.

The one thing that you can definitely anticipate is that meeting a birth parent will never be the way you imagine it will be. There will always be surprises—and that is both good and bad. However, if you are prepared for the unexpected, you will do just fine. For some adoptees it is very important that they meet their birth parents; for others it is just not an issue.

Let's back up a bit first. You say that you want to meet your birth parents. Depending on the nature of your adoption (whether it was an agency adoption or a private adoption through an attorney, doctor, or third party) there may be different requirements that you must fulfill prior to actually meeting a birth parent. These requirements may come from state law or be the established policies of an adoption agency.

Some agencies, for example, require that you reach legal adulthood prior to initiating any kind of contact. Other agencies will allow a minor to make limited contact—such as writing a letter—with the permission of the adoptive parents. There are agencies that require that a certain number of letters be exchanged prior to actual contact or that all parties involved participate in counseling as a first step prior to actually meeting one another. All agencies have policies that they must follow as part of their original agreement with the biological parents and the adoptive family. It is likely that your parents know the agency's policies and could discuss these with you.

If your adoption was a private adoption, it may be more difficult for you to make contact. Many private adoptions are handled by lawyers or doctors who pledge absolute confidentiality to their clients. This means that they cannot disclose any information to the adoptee unless the birth parent requested contact at the time of the adoption. Additionally, people retire, offices close, and records are often difficult to find so many years after the original adoption took place. So, in order to "prepare" yourself for an initial meeting, the adoptee must first determine what requirements need to be met in order to make some type of contact with his or her birth parents.

I would encourage you to involve your adoptive parents early in the process. Talk to them about your feelings and why you want to meet your birth parents at this time in your life. Then your parents can help you to process your concerns. Are you looking for medical information? Do you wonder how tall you will be or why you struggle in certain subjects at school? Some adopted teens want to know why an adoption plan was made for them.

Whatever questions or concerns you have, be assured that other adopted teens have many of the same questions. Some agencies do, in fact, provide support groups for adopted people where they can share their concerns and issues regarding adoption. These groups can be very helpful in clarifying what issues are most important to you. There are also some community support groups that provide a place where adopted children, birth parents, and adoptive parents come together to process their issues and to provide support to one another before, during, and after a search is made.

Read everything you can about the adoption process. There are many good books available to you at your local library. Adoption involves an intense emotional journey for everyone in the triad: the birth parents, the adoptive parents, and the adoptee. Before you begin your journey, you need to understand more fully how adoption impacts birth parents and adoptive parents as well. (This is one time when it is really not all about you!) Adopted teens should try to be sensitive to the feelings of everyone.

Meeting a birth parent is really the culmination of a long process emotionally. It certainly involves more than simply locating a birth parent in a particular city or state. Your preparation for this important event needs to consider the many

"As I stood on the subway traveling from Seoul to Inchon, where I was meeting my birth father, I broke down and started to sob. My friend Trilika, a mixed black and Korean adoptee, looked at me and said, 'Hollee, you are making more room.' And I realized that was what I had to do. When you meet your birth family, you are taking on more, not less. You open yourself up to a family that you may not remember and yet is yours by birth. You must decide how much of your life you want to share with them."[3]
—Hollee McGinnis, Policy and Operations Director, Evan B. Donaldson Adoption Institute

people involved in your adoption. And most importantly, you must prepare yourself psychologically for actually meeting the people who gave you your biological roots.

Should I contact my birth parents ahead of time before I drop in to meet them?

You can drop in on your best friend and you can drop in on your grandmother, but you should absolutely not "drop in" on a birth parent. Meeting a birth parent for the first time is a momentous occasion in both your lives and is a time in which everyone involved should be prepared.

Have you ever thrown yourself together and run out to the mall only to run into an old girlfriend? At a time when you wanted to look your very best, you may have been wearing tattered jeans and having a "bad hair day." For the rest of the day you may have felt that you made a terrible impression on your friend. You wouldn't want to put your birth parent in that embarrassing situation.

Meeting a birth parent is more than simply coming face-to-face with a stranger. It is very likely that your birth parent has thought of you on every birthday, every Mother's Day, every Father's Day—maybe even every day of his or her life. A contact should always be made in advance. If you are working with an agency, it is likely that the agency will make all of the arrangements for your first meeting. Agencies always try to be very discreet when they contact a birth parent because other important people in the birth parent's life (a spouse, a child, another relative) may not know that you exist. Remember, your adoption took place many years ago. Most birth parents go on to build a new life for themselves. It would be very insensitive of an adoptee to arrive on a birth parent's doorstep without notice. It could be very awkward or even embarrassing to the birth parent and would be a difficult way to begin an important meeting.

How will my adoptive parents react when I go to meet my birth parents?

We have talked about meeting birth parents as a journey. Since you are seventeen years old and a minor, your adoptive parents are an important part of the process of meeting your biological parents. In fact, your quest begins an emotional journey for your adoptive parents as well. It is so important that you are all together on this journey. You are, after all, a family.

Everyone on this earth has two kinds of parents: biological parents and psychological parents. Biological parents are the mother and father who provide us with our genetic makeup. Biological parents determine our height, hair color, eye color, temperament, and natural abilities. We may have our birth mother's eyes and our paternal great-grandfather's nose. Thousands of generations of genes from our biological parents come together at the moment of conception to create a unique new person, you. You have never existed before and no one exactly like you will ever exist again.

Psychological parents, on the other hand, are the parents who raise us and help to shape our values, beliefs, and behaviors. They give us our traditions and help us to grow and develop into who we are. They do not form us physically, but they do shape us emotionally. For most people, the biological and psychological parents are the same people. For people who are adopted, however, there is a major difference. An adopted person's biological parents are one set of parents, their birth parents. The adopted person's psychological parents are their adoptive parents.

Even though your adoptive parents did not give birth to you, they know you better than any other people in your life. They began their own psychological journey into adoption long before you were born, and perhaps even before you were conceived. Hopefully, they have continued to discuss adoption with you throughout your life. They have probably discussed with one another how they would feel about you meeting your birth parents one day.

There is no way to know how your adoptive parents will feel about your wish to meet your birth parents. The only way that you will understand how they feel is to talk to them about your desire to meet your birth parents. Some adoptive parents might be surprised, some may feel hurt; others will be very open to learning about your wish to meet birth parents.

Sometimes adoptive parents feel that they have loved their child from the very first contact, and they do not understand why you would want to meet the people who created you. In every respect except for conception, your adoptive parents are your "real" parents. They might feel that you are in some way rejecting them in favor of your birth parents. They may even fear that you would leave them to move in with a birth parent! Although this is seldom the reality, your parents' feelings are very real, and as a young adult, you do need to respect their feelings. Generally, adopted teens who search for birth parents are looking for their roots; they are not looking for parents, because they already have them.

The most important thing is to talk to your parents and listen to their input. They might ask you to wait a bit longer or to participate in counseling or a support group before going any further with your search. They may be thrilled with your decision and offer to help you to work through the details. The point is that at your age (you are still a minor), your parents are your best allies in your quest. Before you do anything else, talk to them. They have wisdom and life experience that is invaluable to you at this time in your life.

Is it better to meet your birth parents alone or with someone? It seems as though it might be a little awkward alone.

This again is a matter of choice. The most important thing to realize is that you are meeting a stranger for the first time, even though this "stranger" is a biological parent. Do not expect that you will feel an immediate connection and that you will be intimate friends. Many adopted teens think that once they meet a birth parent, there will be an automatic melding of minds and hearts. This is probably not true. Your relationship to your birth parent is biological. So, in every respect except for biology, you are complete strangers.

You should seriously consider meeting your birth parent for the first time with your adoptive parents present. (This is not the time, incidentally, to bring along your best friend.) Certainly it could be awkward meeting a birth parent alone. If the meeting has been arranged by an adoption agency, an attorney, or a doctor, it is likely that this professional will want to be a part of your first meeting together. This is a good time to listen to that internal voice you have that helps you to make good decisions. If you feel that meeting a birth parent alone would be awkward (and most adopted teens would agree with you!), then arrange your first meeting with your adoptive parents by your side.

How should I act when I meet my birth parents? Do I ask questions about my heritage, their lives, or what sort of things should we converse about?

This is an excellent question and one that is often not discussed in books about adoption. The most important thing is that you be genuine when you meet your birth parent for the first time. This is not the time to be anyone but yourself—and the very best that you can be. Remember that you are probably as nervous as your birth parent! Just as you might worry about what your birth parent will think of you, you can be assured that your birth parent is thinking the very same thing. Many birth mothers fear that their adopted child will not like them or will be angry with them because of the adoption. Some adopted teens, on the other hand, often fear rejection by the birth parent due to feelings that maybe they were placed for adoption because there was something "wrong" with them.

Think about all that you have learned about meeting people in the past and use this knowledge when you meet your birth parents. There are many levels of conversation, from very superficial to very personal. It is best to begin your conversation with more impersonal questions that would not be upsetting to your birth parent.

You might begin your meeting by telling your birth parent how much it means to you to finally meet. Thank this person for giving you this opportunity and perhaps even more importantly, for giving you the gift of life. The conversation should flow naturally from that point. Your biological mother might ask you about your school and what you enjoy studying. She might ask you about your family or your special interests and aptitudes. Both you and your birth parent should have many questions for one another.

Avoid asking very personal questions at this first meeting. Your birth parent may tell you something about her situation at the time of the adoption and the reasons why an adoption plan was made for you. On the other hand, this information could also be quite painful to discuss with you, a stranger, at a first meeting. You will need to be sensitive to the feelings of everyone involved.

Certainly you may ask about things that are important to you that you have wondered about. Do you want to know about your nationality or medical history? This would be a good time to ask those questions. Remember that your birth parent will also probably have questions for you. It is likely that he or she has wondered about you for as long, or longer, than you have wondered about him or her.

Listen carefully to what your birth parent tells you and use that as a springboard for your questions. Above all, be sensitive to how very emotional this meeting might be for everyone involved. It is always better to say less than more in such a delicate situation. You do not want to bombard your birth parent with questions or with information about yourself. There will be time for that in the future if you mutually decide to maintain a relationship.

It seems to me that the best place to meet would be in a public place, but what would be the best place to meet? A public place or a more private setting such as the birth parents' house?

If your reunion is arranged by your adoption agency, it is likely that your first meeting will take place at the agency. Some agencies arrange the first meeting and then ask the family if they would like to go out together for lunch or dinner. Other agencies insist that all meetings take place at the agency itself in order to maintain some confidentiality for everyone involved.

If you are meeting a birth parent outside of the agency, it might be best to find a restaurant that is somewhat quiet for your first meeting. Imagine how difficult it would be to try to discuss personal information in a place that is noisy or one with constant interruptions. Talk to your parents about finding a location that is both pleasant and somewhat private. It is not a good idea to meet at your home or at the home of the birth parent. You are looking for an emotionally "neutral" location where everyone feels comfortable.

After we meet, what should my relationship be with my birth parents? Do I keep in touch or visit them occasionally?

Everyone involved (you, your birth parent, your parents) needs to make a decision about where your relationship will proceed from this point on. You may feel

Tips for a Successful First Meeting with Birth Parents

1. Consider choosing a neutral place to first meet, a casual restaurant, for example. If either one of you becomes uncomfortable during the meeting, you will be able to leave easily. If everyone is having a good time, you can order dessert and linger.

2. Each of you probably wants to bring along one person to keep you company and help the conversation. But keep it simple. Don't bring all the aunts and uncles. You might ask her not to bring her four kids to that first meeting. If possible, use that meeting to let the two of you get acquainted. You can decide if you want to meet all the other relatives later.

3. Make a small photo album with a few pictures for each year of your life since you've been apart. Use scanned copies of pictures, so you can give your birth mom or family member the copy if you wish. This album will give you something to look at and talk about if you get nervous and tongue-tied. Making the photo album is a fun and reassuring project you can work on with your mom or dad.[4]

4. Plan ahead that the first meeting will last an hour or two. Otherwise, the meeting can go on and on. People may be afraid to end the meeting but may really get wiped out emotionally if it goes on too long. Remember, you might be able to get together again. If one of you is from out of town, you may plan several time-limited meetings over a period of a day or two. If you like each other, you can always let the time together go a little longer.

5. Assuming you are okay with each other, decide how you will get in touch next and who makes the next move. Birth parents often talk about how scared they are after a reunion. They fear the adopted person won't like them and will disappear from their life again. This agreement to stay in touch can be simple. "Is it okay if I e-mail you before the end of the week? I'd love to hear from you once you've had time to think." If you keep it slow, these relationships can grow more normally and have a better chance of lasting longer.

that you would like to maintain contact with your birth parent by phone calls, letters, e-mails, or regular meetings. Some people keep in touch with their birth parents at holidays or birthdays. Others decide that they want to maintain ongoing contact. Keep in mind that your birth parent may have other ideas about any future reunions. This is the time to listen to input from everyone involved and work out a plan that is mutually agreeable to all. You, your birth parent, and your adoptive parents must be comfortable with the type of contact you choose. Relationships involve a process that evolves and changes over time.

You may feel that you now have met your birth parent and that you have no further need to explore this relationship. What if your birth parent feels differently? These are questions that need to be processed before your first meeting. Again, it would be very helpful if you and your adoptive parents were involved in a support group where you might learn about all the different outcomes and feelings that others have experienced when meeting with a birth parent. This vicarious experience will help you to deal with the reality of meeting your birth parent. You must remain as flexible as possible, because you will not know how things will proceed until you actually make contact.

Very often adopted teens have a "fantasy" birth parent in mind when they begin their search. A fantasy birth parent is usually a "perfect" parent—one who will truly understand them, who will listen to their innermost feelings with sensitivity and never say no to them. Fantasy birth parents do not set curfews or place restrictions on their teens. They never lose their temper. They look like models and are totally immersed in the culture and language of the adolescent. They are all gourmet cooks, have never struggled with weight issues, and are brilliant, articulate, and financially stable. Unfortunately, fantasy birth parents do not exist in reality. All parents—biological and adoptive—are less than perfect. In meeting your birth parent for the first time, you must be prepared to meet a very real human being with strengths and weaknesses, a person who loved you enough to make an adoption plan for you so that you could have the life that the birth parent could not give you.

You may discover that you have many things in common with a birth parent. You may both love pizza or excel in mathematics. On the other hand, you may be disappointed to learn that you can find few similarities between you and your biological parent. How can that be? We are all the composite not only of thousands of generations of genes, but also of our life experiences. The person you are and the biological parent you meet may have grown up in completely different worlds. It will take time for you to truly understand one another and to appreciate the differences that you each bring to your initial meeting.

As you can see, the subject of meeting a birth parent is extremely complex. It must be approached with sensitivity, maturity, flexibility, and empathy. Your

While chances are slim that many adopted teens will discover that they have a famous birth mother, there are several movie and television stars who have placed babies in adoptive homes for various reasons. These birth mothers later reunited with the children they placed for adoption.

Roseanne Barr is a well-known actress and comedian. She starred in the long-running TV comedy *Roseanne*. Before Roseanne got married for the first time in 1974, she gave birth to a baby girl and placed her for adoption. Roseanne met her birth daughter in later years and still has some contact with her.[5]

Joni Mitchell is a Grammy award-winning singer and songwriter and has recorded numerous rock and jazz albums. Joni gave up a baby girl for adoption in 1965 when she was twenty-one years old. At that time, Joni was not married and had very little income. Shortly after she placed her baby for adoption, her singing career took off. In 1971 Joni released a song about the daughter she placed, named Kelly. The song was titled "Little Green," for the color kelly green. The song talks about Joni being sad and sorry, but not ashamed of placing her daughter. The lyrics also wish her daughter a happy ending. Joni's daughter was named Kilauren by her adoptive parents. Kilauren was not told she was adopted until she was twenty-seven. Once she found out she had a birth mother, Kilauren began to search for her. After five years, Kilauren found her birth mother, the then very famous Joni Mitchell.[6]

Faith Ireland served as a superior court judge for fifteen years. She was then elected to the Supreme Court of Washington state. When Faith was twenty-two, she became pregnant while still in college. Unmarried at the time, she gave birth to a daughter in 1964 and placed her for adoption. Faith was reunited with her daughter in 1997.[7]

Kate Mulgrew, an actress probably most famous for her role in *Star Trek: Voyager*, has also acted in nine movies and thirty television shows. In 1977, while she appeared on the soap opera *Ryan's Hope*, she became pregnant. Kate was not married at the time and placed her daughter with an adoptive family. Kate met her biological daughter in 2001.[8]

Mercedes Ruehl won an Academy Award for Best Supporting Actress in the movie *The Fisher King* in 1992. She is also well-known for playing Tom Hanks' mother in the movie *Big*. When she was twenty-eight, Mercedes placed a baby boy for adoption. She felt she wasn't mature enough and didn't have enough money to raise a child. She later met her son when he turned twenty-one. In 1997 Mercedes and her husband adopted a baby boy, Javier.[9]

adoptive parents can be an incredible asset to you as you journey into the world of adoptive reunions. Involve them early in the process. Preparation is absolutely essential to a successful reunion. Immerse yourself in reading about adoption reunions, get involved in a support group, and find a therapist with a background in adoption to guide you on your journey. This is truly a momentous occasion in your life.

The Moment of Truth

Sometimes when a birth parent is reunited with his or her child, something wonderful, almost magical happens—an instant, unexplainable connection occurs. Emotions are honestly shared and received. An unbreakable, lifelong bond is created. For others, a first meeting may be a bit awkward or frightening at first, but after everyone relaxes, a comfortable relationship begins to form. As time goes on the birth parent and child slowly figure out how this new relationship will fit in their existing lives.

Unfortunately, not all reunions go as planned, and some result in bitter feelings, severe disappointment, or other negative emotions. When one adoptee, Sarah, found her birth mother, she faced a major letdown when their relationship didn't turn out as she had hoped.

My Story: Sarah

"I was adopted when I was six weeks old by a loving couple living in a small, conservative town in Indiana. Two years later they had a biological son, my brother Scott. Although my parents are great, I never felt I shared the same bond with them as my brother. For some reason I believed that if they had known they could have had a baby of their own, they never would have wanted me. Perhaps I felt this way because I sensed I was different from my parents in many ways. My brother and parents seemed to have this easy, very natural connection.

"Growing up, my parents always told me that I was special because there were 'four people who loved me very much.' Although I perceived I was different from my parents, I never doubted that they did love me, yet I always dreamed about finding these other two people. I wondered if I might have more in common with them. My adoptive parents made a standing offer that whenever I was ready to find my birth parents, they would help me. When I was around sixteen years old, I decided I wanted to meet my birth mom. I visualized her as this really cool person with whom I would have a close relationship. My fantasy was that she would be like Madonna. In my sixteen-year-old world, Madonna was the ultimate in cool. I hoped that when my birth mother and I met, we would share the special bond I longed for.

"Sensing I wasn't quite ready to meet my birth mom at sixteen, I didn't act on this decision until several years later. When I was twenty-one, my parents again asked if I wanted their help in finding my birth parents, and this time I said 'yes.' It was a rather simple process to locate my birth mother. First my parents opened my adoption records. Then I was told to write a letter to my birth mother and explain that I wished to meet her and give her my contact information. I soon got word that my birth mother agreed to meet me, but I had to wait for her to contact me—that was the rule. It was very stressful waiting because I never knew when she might call. In hindsight, I wish I would have had more control over the situation and had been more prepared.

"I was away at college when my birth mother called. Almost immediately we began to talk about what we looked like and discussed similarities. Standing at 5'8", I always felt tall. I discovered my birth mother was a whopping 6'1"! We quickly made plans to meet at her home. It was about a six- to seven-hour drive from school, so she insisted on paying for a hotel room where I could stay. My parents offered to go with me, but I felt guilty about wanting to meet her. I felt it might hurt my parents' feelings if they went with me, so I asked a friend to make the trip instead.

"My friend dropped me at my birth mother's home with the agreement she would come back to get me when I called. As I got out of the car, my birth mother, Peg, came out of the house to greet me. We were both crying by the time we reached each other. Immediately I was taken by Peg's appearance. She was tall and very tan with striking blonde hair. As we walked back into her trailer home, I sensed she was indeed cool. She even had a Cleveland Indians tattoo on her back. I was happy to finally meet her, but I remember my overriding emotion was excitement. I was very thrilled to learn about this piece of my history that had been a mystery to me for so long. I hoped to find I had some half-siblings but was disappointed to learn I was the only child Peg had ever had. It seemed she was not interested in being a mother. The more we talked, the more I realized she wasn't really the 'mother' type at all. I was surprised to find that she kept a tanning bed in the spare room of the small house where she lived alone.

"At first I enjoyed introducing my college friends to my 'cool' birth mother. As time went on and we shared about our past, I learned that Peg had had a rough life. I met Peg's parents, my biological grandparents, and found it was easier to relate to my grandmother than Peg. I enjoy relationships that are honest and real, but I found I couldn't get past the surface with Peg. It seemed I couldn't trust the things she said. Over time her behavior appeared rather dysfunctional. One thing that separated us was the fact that Peg would not tell me the name of my birth father. Sometimes, after pressing her for details, she would give me a first name, but these always turned out to be false leads. In the end, I decided my birth mother's unstable behavior, and the relationship we had developed, were not healthy for me. Even though I didn't find what I had hoped for, I'm glad my questions about my birth mother are answered. And I hope that sometime in the future I will be able to find that fourth person, who, I've been told, 'loves me very much.' But no matter what happens, I will always have my mom and dad, who truly make me feel special, because I know they love me very much."[10]

What about You?

As you prepare to meet your birth parents, it's a good idea to spend some time thinking about the reasons why you want to meet them. You may also want to do a "reality check" and make sure you haven't been dreaming up some unrealistic fantasies about your birth parents and how your life might have been different if you hadn't been adopted.

Then the time will finally come when all the planning and preparing are finished, and you will finally meet your birth parent—an event that you will have

Movie: *August Rush*

In the 2007 movie *August Rush*, an orphaned boy named Evan (played by Freddie Highmore), displays extraordinary musical talent at a young age. After discovering the boy's ability to play the guitar, a crafty street dweller (played by Robin Williams) renames the boy "August Rush" and attempts to make money off his talent. In the dramatic ending, the boy's musical gift helps him reunite with his birth parents.

visualized many times in your mind. Relax and relish the moment. Enjoy learning about this person who was a part of giving you life. Hear his or her story. Tell your story. Ask the questions that have followed you for so many years. Get the answers you need. And remember, for the most part your birth parent is who he or she is. You are who you are. And none of you can change the past. Focus on moving forward and making the most of your future ahead.

Discussion Questions

Are you interested in meeting your birth parents at some point? Why?

If so, do you think it might be easier to talk to birth parents on the phone before meeting them? Why?

Would you want to set any personal boundaries or limits before you meet your birth parents?

Where do you think would be the best place to meet a birth parent the first time?

Who would you want to be with you if you met your birth parents?

What's the most important thing you'd like to tell your birth parents?

What would you most hope to gain by meeting your birth mother or father?

What would you do if you could not accomplish that goal during your meeting?

Notes

1. Billy, e-mail correspondence, April 10, 2006.
2. Andrew, e-mail correspondence, March 17, 2006.
3. Hollee McGinnis, e-mail correspondence, December 5, 2006.
4. Adoption Learning Partners, "Lifebooks: Creating and Telling Your Child's Story," www .adoptionlearningpartners.org/courses/lifebooks.cfm (accessed July 31, 2006).
5. Adoption.com, "Birth Parent Biographies," celebrities.adoption.com/famous/birth-parent -bios.html (accessed February 16, 2006).
6. Brian D. Johnson, "Joni's Secret: Mother and Child Reunion" *MacLean's* (April 21, 1997), jmdl.com/library/view.cfm?id=91 (accessed February 16, 2006).
7. Adoption.com, "Birth Parent Biographies," celebrities.adoption.com/famous/faith-ireland .html (accessed February 16, 2006).
8. Adoption.com, "Birth Parent Biographies," celebrities.adoption.com/famous/kate-mulgrew .html (accessed February 16, 2006).
9. *Yahoo! Movies*, "Mercedes Ruehl," movies.yahoo.com/movie/contributor/1800019603/bio (accessed February 16, 2006).
10. Sarah, telephone interview, July 10, and e-mail correspondence July 13 and August 5, 2006.

INTERNATIONAL ADOPTIONS

"I had the opportunity of a lifetime back in fifth grade. On December 5, 1997, I left on a nineteen-hour plane ride back to India, where I was born. I spent two weeks there with my mom and a tour group. I had an amazing time and visited six cities.

"One of those cities was Calcutta. Calcutta was very crowded. I was able to go back to I.M.H., the hospital where I was born, and take a tour. I met the nurse who took care of me when I was there at three months old. She was surprised and very happy to see me. I was surprised she was still there and actually remembered me with all of the babies she has taken care of. We did not have a whole lot of time, and she was pretty busy so I wasn't able to visit with her as much as I would have hoped, but that was all right.

"Going back to India was an amazing experience and it made me feel how fortunate I really am. I saw some sad things there, like the overwhelmingly large poverty population. For some people there, just surviving is a challenge, while most people here in the United States have it made. I don't take school for granted anymore, but I still could do better at my school habits. I often think about the trip and can't believe it has been as long as it has since I went there. When I came back from that trip, I kept looking back and thinking how different my life would be if I lived there."[1]—Ben, age 19

Sometimes people travel thousands of miles, and even across vast oceans, to become part of a new family. A family that includes an internationally adopted child is created this way. But as the years pass by, some children who were born in other countries begin to have questions about where they were born, their heritage, and the birth parents they left behind. They may know a few basic answers but would like to find out more details about their background. Many internationally adopted children often wonder who took care of them before they were placed, or what their life would be like if they had grown up where they were born. They question why they were placed and wonder how their birth parents are doing now.

Your Questions

As a teen adopted from another country, you may have been wondering about certain questions for years. Some of these may revolve around your birth parents and the reasons they placed you. Common explanations for international adoptions include poverty, famine, war, or other socioeconomic problems. Many birth parents choose adoption to ensure the safety of their children. You may find it helpful to investigate the conditions in the country where you were born that could have affected your birth mother and possibly her decision to place you for adoption.

Don't Feel Guilty

If you discover that the situation in your birth country was less than ideal during the time you were placed, it can be tempting to feel guilty that you escaped possible harm. You didn't have a choice about leaving your birth country and therefore had nothing to do with the fact that you avoided a potentially dangerous upbringing where there was fighting, hunger, or hardship. Learning about the conditions in your birth country may also cause you to become concerned about the well-being of your birth parents. To help alleviate those fears, ask your parents if they received any letters or updates about your birth parents through the years. You could also try contacting the agency in the country that placed you. It may be a bit of a long shot, but perhaps someone there would have informa-

Finding Miracles, by Julia Alvarez (published by Knopf in 2004), is a compelling novel about a teen named Milly Kaufman who was adopted from South America. Growing up in Vermont, Milly likes the fact that she looks like most other American teens and can easily blend in with others. When a new boy, Pablo Bolivar, moves into the area, Milly's life becomes more complicated. Pablo has come from Milly's native country. Eventually Milly's friends discover that she is adopted, and she must face the heritage she has long denied. This turn of events prompts Milly to take a trip back to her birth country, where she discovers the true meaning of "home" in this book, which addresses the topics of family, friendship, and heritage.

tion about your birth parents and can reassure you they are okay. If they aren't in contact with your birth parents, don't assume the worst. Adoption agencies, especially those that place thousands of babies overseas each year, may find it difficult to keep track of the many birth parents they serve.

Traditions and Cultures

Certain traditions and cultural standards are other reasons behind many international adoptions. Adoptions that stem from these reasons are sometimes difficult for Americans to fully understand. In Korea, for example, a family registry for each male is carefully maintained. Each man's registry lists all of his children. If an unmarried woman gives birth, her child's name will not be placed on the biological father's registry because he is not married to the birth mother. This child cannot become a full member of Korean society because he or she is not listed on a registry. As a result, children born out of wedlock in Korea are often placed for adoption in another country. Koreans place a strong emphasis on the importance of blood relatives, which makes adoptions within the country very unusual.

China's "one-child" policy, enacted in the 1970s, is another reason many birth mothers overseas ended up placing their babies in the United States and other countries. While some exceptions are occasionally granted, this policy usually allows each family to have only one child. The communist government of China created this policy to slow its rapidly growing population. Over the years, the government has routinely carried out forced abortions and sterilizations and refused to pay for education and/or medical benefits for "second" children. Thousands of "second" babies in China have been adopted by families in the United States. Recently China has begun to rethink its one-child policy. In fact, in the year 2000, the government initiated a plan to phase it out in the future.[2]

"Research on Korean adoptees who search for their biological parents indicates that all adoptees gradually become interested in different kinds of searches. Motivated by our interest in learning more about our roots, our first search is typically for our birth culture. Lastly, after possibly visiting our birth country, we may consider the possibility of searching for and reuniting with birth parents. Often a search is about the journey of searching and not the actual reunion. So it is important to understand what it is you seek."[3]—Hollee McGinnis, Policy and Operations Director, Evan B. Donaldson Adoption Institute

Royal Blood

Wouldn't it be cool if you found out you were really a prince or a princess and you had loyal subjects in your native country that awaited your return? Sarah Culberson, an African American who was adopted by a Caucasian couple when she was one year-old, later discovered she was indeed a princess. And she had 36,000 subjects living in Sierra Leone, Africa!

Growing up in her adoptive home, Sarah often wondered about her birth parents and her heritage, but she never dreamed she had a royal background. Although she was a biracial child in the predominantly white community of Morgantown, West Virginia, Sarah felt accepted and loved. Her adoptive father, Jim, was a college professor, and her mother, Judy, taught at an elementary school. Sarah describes her childhood as happy, but she does admit there were times when she worked hard to feel like she fit in.

When Sarah was eighteen she began searching for her birth parents. She soon learned that her birth mother had died from cancer when Sarah was around ten. Saddened by this news, and fearing that her biological father would not want to meet her, Sarah decided not to continue her search to find him. In 2001, Sarah moved to California to study acting with the hopes of starting a career in that field. While taking a class in personal growth, Sarah discovered she had a

genuine fear of being rejected by her birth father. Deciding it was finally time to overcome that fear, Sarah hired a private investigator to look for her father. That same day, the investigator provided her with an address in Maryland where he suspected her father was living.

Sarah wrote her father a note that included her cell phone number and dropped it in the mail. Unfortunately, the address she had been given was actually the home of her father's brother. Sarah's uncle passed her information to her father, Joseph Kposowa, who lived in an African village of Bumpe, population 2,000. Joseph was thrilled to receive news about his daughter. He quickly drove his old car to the town of Bo where he could use a phone and call his daughter. Sarah was taking a walk outside when she received his call.

Joseph told Sarah who he was and explained that he was sorry he hadn't been able to find her in all these years. He said that since Sarah's parents had changed her name when they adopted her, he had not been able to locate her. Sarah's birth father also answered one of her deepest questions when he provided details about her adoption. Joseph had met Sarah's birth mother when he came to West Virginia as a visiting college student. The two became close and soon found themselves facing an unplanned pregnancy. They both decided that they were too young and did not have enough money to raise a child.

After some discussion, Sarah was very pleased to find she had a caring birth father and surprised to learn of her royal heritage. Her father invited her to come and visit Africa and meet the people who belonged to her chiefdom. Sarah flew to Sierra Leone in December 2004. Her father met her at the airport. Joseph gave Sarah a traditional African dress, which she wore the next day when she traveled to Bumpe. Hundreds of villagers welcomed Sarah with a song they had written especially for her. The women sang the song in their native language called Mende. Many women fought to hug and kiss Sarah as they sang their "Welcome home" song. Sarah was seated at the head table next to her uncle, the paramount chief. She was given the name "Bumpe-nya," which means Lady of Bumpe.

Sarah enjoyed meeting the people of Bumpe, but she soon discovered that all was not well in this town. During her visit in Africa, she learned of the horrible civil war that had been raging in the area for the past eleven years. Enemies had attacked Bumpe and killed villagers. They had also ruthlessly cut off the hands of many others so they would not be able to fight. Houses and other buildings had been destroyed. The people who survived were very poor, living on about $50 each month. The situation was very serious and seemed overwhelming to Sarah.

After she returned to the United States, Sarah struggled with what she should do. She felt obligated to help her tribe and guilty about her comfortable, easy life. She soon began to receive phone calls from desperate Bumpe villagers who pleaded for money and her help. One of Sarah's friends decided to start the Kposowa Foundation, named after Sarah's birth father. This nonprofit organization (found at www.bumpefund.com) helps raise money for the needs of the people in Africa. By helping to organize events that raise money for the foundation, Sarah is helping her people and is acting as a true princess should.[4]

In some cultures, it is completely unacceptable to have a child if you are not married. Single parenthood is unheard of in many countries. In societies that hold these beliefs, unplanned pregnancies for single women usually end in abortion or adoption. In countries where only men are allowed to have a job and earn money, many women are forced to make difficult decisions when their husbands die. A widow may place her children, even after she has raised them for years, in order to attract a new husband. Remarriage is her only possible source of income to buy the necessities she needs to survive.

Passing Judgment

It can be easy to make a harsh judgment about societies that are very different from ours, particularly those that seem to neglect young children or enforce rules that seem unfair. As you learn about your birth country, make sure you dig into the details to gain a fuller understanding of the religious or political reasons behind the traditions and ideas that may have led to your placement. By gaining knowledge about your birth parents' true situation, you may be better equipped to genuinely understand their reasons for choosing adoption. And whether you agree with those reasons or not, at least knowing them may help you move beyond criticism to acceptance.

Sense of Self

The teenage years are the time when most people develop their "sense of self," or an understanding of who they really are. Surrounded primarily by people and a culture that are different than your birth country, you may feel a deep desire to understand where you came from as you try to develop your sense of self. Researching the culture, traditions, and religions in your country of origin may be a very helpful part of that process. Knowing your cultural background is beneficial for you as you mature and move forward in your life. It can help you as you learn, face challenges, and make new relationships. A strong sense of self can help you achieve a healthy self-esteem and feel proud and positive about who you are. This will give you confidence as you pursue your goals and dreams.

More Like Me

Learning about your heritage is another useful way to gain a better sense of who you are. One place to start is by searching for a support group of kids who were adopted from the same country you were. Try checking your phone book or doing

Before the Immigration and Nationality Act of 1961 was passed, many people used proxy adoptions to adopt children internationally. This was a popular and highly publicized method for adopting children in which a U.S. couple wanting to adopt from another country would have another person, called a proxy agent, stand in their place during the adoption proceedings in a foreign court. After the child was legally adopted by the couple, the child would be flown to the United States to be united with his or her new parents. These types of adoptions were not subject to the state law requirements and therefore were not always properly monitored. Parents who participated in proxy adoptions were not required to meet any minimum standards as would be expected in an international adoption today. Adoptive families did not need to have any knowledge of the child's culture, such as religious practices, language, eating or sleeping habits, or even the most basic information about the child's home country. They were also not given any training on how to care for children with special needs, or how to prepare for a child who had spent a great deal of time in an orphanage.[5]

an Internet search for a group in your area. You can also connect with teens from other cultures. They may share many of your same challenges and experiences.

Taking a Trip

Some teens have found visiting the country where they were born to be helpful. Immersing yourself in your native culture can be a very meaningful and life-changing experience. It can help you gain a better understanding of your heritage and at the same time gain a new appreciation for the advantages of your current family situation and the country where you live. Each adoption journey is different and very personal. Some may choose travel to their birth country to learn about their heritage, while others may be motivated to make the trip in order to search for birth parents or other blood relatives. Talk about your reasons with your parents. Share your thoughts with your close friends or other internationally adopted teens. Then decide if and when a trip to your first homeland would be beneficial for you.

Teens Talk

Ben, Age 19

"When I went on a trip with my parents to India, people noticed right away that my parents are not Indian like me. They asked what it was like to be adopted and

Closer to Home

If cost, your schedule, or other factors prevent you from taking a trip to your birth country, you could take a heritage trip right here in the United States. You can soak up some culture and great food in many cities in America. For example, there is a very large Russian community located at Brighton Beach in New York. How about a sunny vacation to Los Angeles, home of Koreatown? Or head to Chicago, the Windy City, and stroll down Devon Avenue, where you will find hundreds of Indian shops and restaurants. Chicago also has special areas called Chinatown and Little Italy. You could experience Mexican fare, artwork, and shops in southern Texas. With a little searching, a taste of your native culture may be closer than you think.

It's a Fact

Although the United States is generally thought of as a "receiving country," about 500 children from America are adopted into other countries each year. Most of these children are placed in Europe and Canada.[6]

I said, 'It's great.' Sometimes people asked me things like, 'They aren't your real parents, so why do you listen to them?' And I would respond and tell them that they have taken care of me, loved me, supported me, and raised me like parents should, and that makes them my parents regardless of who gave birth to me. Just like all kids, I have rules and expectations to abide by, so for the most part I do.

"A lot of people were impressed to see how I treated my parents and how well we interacted. They would even tell me that they wished they had my parents and even say that when they have kids, they want them to be like me. It was a strange feeling to have someone my age be telling me these things, but it felt good."[1]

Strength through Diversity

One of the strengths of the United States is that it is made up of many nationalities, races, and cultures. This diverse nation was created from the large number of people who emigrated here in the past, those who continue to emigrate to the United States every year, and also through international adoptions. Recent data shows that children arriving in the United States to be adopted come from twenty different countries. Here's a look at the number of children adopted from various countries into the United States in 2006[7]:

- China (mainland)—6,493
- Guatemala—4,135
- Russia—3,706
- South Korea—1,376
- Ethiopia—732
- Kazakhstan—587
- Ukraine—460
- Liberia—353
- Colombia—344
- India—320
- Haiti—309
- Philippines—245
- China (born in Taiwan)—187

Off the Bookshelf

The Lost Daughters of China (published in 2000) is a book that explores China's history of placing thousands of its own daughters for adoption and the underlying causes, China's one-child policy, and the cultural emphasis placed on having male children. The author, Karen Evans, adopted a one-year-old girl from China in 1997, and has studied the surge of adopting Chinese girls in the United States that began in the late 1980s. This book examines the complex issues of a child being abandoned by one culture and raised in another.

- Vietnam—163
- Mexico—70
- Poland—67
- Brazil—66
- Nepal—66
- Nigeria—62
- Thailand—56

Understanding Others

Michael, age seventeen, was born in Guatemala and now lives happily in New Jersey with his adoptive family. Michael finds that people often make false assumptions about his heritage based on his appearance. He shares the comments he often hears: "I tend to get questions like, 'Are you Mexican?' or 'Are you Puerto Rican?' and I respond to them, 'No, I am Guatemalan.' Many people are ignorant and have no idea about other cultures, and tend to think everyone who looks like me is Mexican, but I understand that. I know that black people, white people, every kind of nationality can be adopted, and I realize that everyone doesn't know about all of the cultures in the world."[8]

Over time, Michael has learned that the insensitive questions he receives from others are often simply the result of ignorance. If you face uncomfortable comments as an internationally adopted teen, it might help you to remember that many people do not know much about the various cultures and ethnic groups in the world. Perhaps you, like Michael, could help broaden others' understanding of human diversity.

Michael is proud of his heritage and shares how he chooses to acknowledge it in his life. "I don't celebrate my heritage on a special day or with a certain event,"

> ## ! It's a Fact
>
> When the Asian Languages and Literatures professors at the University of Minnesota noticed that about 30 percent of the students who were studying Korean were adoptees, they created a brand-new class called "Cultures of Korean Adoptions: The Adoptee Experience." This breakthrough course is the first class offered in the United States that gives college-age adoptees an academic forum to discuss adoption and its effect on their lives. The class covers many important topics to adoptees, such as U.S. and international adoption policies.[9]

Michael says, "but I do make sure that everyone knows what nationality I am. I celebrate my culture when I speak about it, and that works great for me."

Teens Ask

Teens who have been adopted from other countries often find it difficult to find answers to questions that relate to their adoption. Katrina Carlisle, an adoption specialist with many years of experience in the adoption field and international adoptions, answers some of the most common questions that internationally adopted teens ask.

How can I find my birth parents since I was born in Russia and I have no adoption records to help me?

> Katrina Carlisle, LSW, BSW, is currently the Adoption Counselor and Adoption Search Specialist at St. Elizabeth Coleman Pregnancy and Adoption Services in Indianapolis, Indiana. Katrina has seventeen years of experience as a social worker in the field of adoption. She has provided services to adoptive parents, birth parents, and adult adoptees and regularly leads transracial adoption seminars. Katrina co-authored the book *Adoption for Dummies*, which is a comprehensive guide to building a family through adoption. Katrina is the parent of a reunited adult adoptee and has been working in the area of search and reunion since 1992.

I would love to reassure you that you will certainly be able find your birth parents, but that would be dishonest. Unfortunately, many people adopted from Russia (and other countries) may never find their birth parents. However, there are some things you can do. Remember you may want to enlist the aid of your parents and you may need to wait until you are older to follow through with some of these suggestions.

First and foremost, find out all the information you can. Ask your parents for copies of all the documents relating to your adoption. Quiz them about additional facts they may have been told (and take notes). Collect photos of the agency office, orphanage, courts, and so on that were used in your adoption overseas. Contact your agency and ask what assistance they offer adoptees in searching for their birth parents.

Contact businessmen and -women in your community that emigrated here from your birth country. Ask them for suggestions on how to gather additional information and what agencies in your home country might be of some help. Ask if they know anyone traveling frequently to your home country that could make some initial inquiries for you. (My own daughter used this method, and a Korean professor was a great help to her in locating information. She had a reunion thanks to his help and the help of our agency in Korea.) You might travel to your home country and use an interpreter to launch your own investigation.

Finally, in some countries it is common to find notices in the local newspapers saying some form of, "I am a female child found at the Such-and-So clinic on

Many countries are accustomed to adoptees returning from the United States in the hopes of finding one or both birth parents. Some countries provide avenues to help in that search. For example, in many Korean newspapers there is a special section devoted to helping reunite Korean children with their birth parents. Ads in these sections list information about a searching adoptee, such as the date the child was adopted, their original Korean name, and any other significant memories the adoptee may have. Birth family members who have placed children check these columns often. There is also a television show that features adoptees who are looking for birth parents in Korea. Adoptees may display early photographs taken when they were placed, or articles of clothing they wore when they arrived in America, during their time slot on the show. Many biological families have been reunited as a result of the cooperative attitude of countries that have sent children to the United States.[10]

9-13-99. I was wearing a yellow gown and was approximately three days old. I am looking for my birth parents."

Is there some way I can find my original birth certificate so I can find the names of my birth parents?

A great way for teens to learn about their heritage and connect with other teens from their native culture is by attending Heritage Camps. These camps are held in different cities around the country for a few days or a week in the summer. Campers spend time learning about the foods, traditions, language, religion, sports, and many other things. There are various camps that feature different countries and cultures. For example, a camp for children adopted from India is held every July in Roselle, Illinois. A group called Heart Adoption Services sponsors a Chinese Heritage Camp in Turner, Ohio, in June. Every August a Russian Heritage Camp is held in Fraser, Colorado.

To find out more about the location of a Heritage Camp for a specific country, try doing a web search using the search words "heritage camp" and then the name of the country. There is also a list of various camps available on the Adoptive Families website, www.AdoptiveFamilies.com. Click on Adoption Events to find a current list of Heritage Camps and other adoption events.[11]

Each country has a different way of handling birth certificates, and unfortunately these methods are also always changing. Some agencies that work with international adoptions send a birth certificate that includes the birth parents' names with the paperwork at the time of the referral. If a birth certificate is not in the original adoption "packet," you may or may not be able to request one later.

I am proud that I was born in another country—it makes me feel special and different. How can I learn more about and celebrate my heritage?

I am happy to hear you want to know more about your cultural heritage. The first thing I would suggest is to talk with your parents about your desire to know more. They may be surprised to hear you have an interest and be eager to learn along with you. Here are some of my ideas.

Many agencies today offer cultural heritage camps for adoptive families. Imagine spending a week with others from the same country in which you were born, eating the food, learning the language, listening to the native music, and learning about customs and celebrations.

Investigate local adoptive family support groups. Many such groups focus on one country only and include educational programs as well as celebrating national holidays, experiencing foods, and even incorporating things such as dance classes for the members.

Use your computer! There is a wealth of information available regarding the cultural traditions of any country. Along this same line, choose your home country as a topic for a school paper. This will force you to do some in-depth research and increase your knowledge.

Subscribe to magazines such as *KoreAm, Chinatown—The Magazine,* and *Russian Life*. Although these magazines target an adult audience, you may really enjoy learning from them. Also, magazines such as *Adoptive Family* include interesting stories about adoptive families traveling to different countries.

If you live in or near a large city, investigate opportunities to meet people native to your country. Are there any festivals celebrated locally? Are there any volunteer opportunities? Are there churches you can visit? Forming friendships with others is a great way to learn. Look around; you will need to be proactive on this one.

Last, and most expensive, homeland tours are a wonderful way to experience your native country with family or friends. Check with your adoption agency for availability, but if nothing is available, check with other agencies or organizations such as support groups.

I think about visiting the country where I was born, but I'm not sure if it's a good idea. How do I know if I should make that trip?

Pass It On

When you discover new things about your heritage, you not only enrich your life, but you gain an important piece of your history that you can pass down to your children someday. If you discover new music, crafts, food, or clothing that you like, you can weave these pieces of your heritage into your daily life. Here are some suggestions for ways to learn more about your native heritage:

- Read about a holiday from your native country and celebrate it with food that is traditionally served that day or with a special ceremony.
- Listen to music that is popular in your country. Look for CDs in you local library or find some on the Internet to download.
- Try your hand at some type of artwork that is prevalent in your home country. Find a local class or buy a book that will help you learn a new craft.
- Investigate the clothing styles commonly worn by others who share your heritage. If you want, make or buy clothes of your own to wear for special occasions.
- Cook up some popular dishes from your homeland. Invite your friends over for a meal and enjoy trying something new together.

Visiting the country of your birth can be a wonderful thing. However, it would not be your typical fun-packed, exciting, family vacation. The key to a successful trip might be something as simple as having realistic expectations. Plan your trip well so you can see the things important to you and yet allow enough down time for journaling, processing, and just some personal reflection. Bring supportive people with you (parents are always good) that will be prepared to hug you when you need it, cry with you, laugh with you, and let you have needed time alone. Expect to be a bundle of mixed emotions as you feel both joy and a sense of loss all at the same time. Overall, this journey can be a time of growth and self-discovery and for some people, a life-changing event.

Toby Dawson won the bronze medal at the 2006 Olympics in the moguls competition in Torino, Italy. This famous skier, nicknamed "Awesome Dawson," was adopted from South Korea. His Korean middle name is Soo Chul, which sounds like "So Cool." Perhaps his cool middle name was foreshadowing his later success in a very cool sport.

As a very young child, Toby was found in front of a police station in South Korea and later placed in an orphanage in Seoul. Although his exact birth date is not known, Toby was around the age of three when he was adopted by a couple from Vail, Colorado. Both of his adoptive parents are ski instructors, and Toby soon caught on to the family sport. He was downhill skiing by age four. Toby has always enjoyed a solid and loving relationship with his adoptive parents.

Growing up, Toby never had a strong desire to find his birth parents, but as a young adult he began to think about searching for them. Toby's worldwide fame

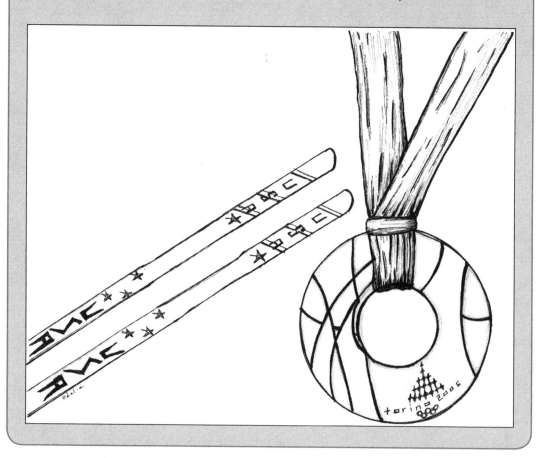

in the 2006 Olympics led to a reunion with his birth father. Following Toby's bronze medal victory in Torino and his public confession that he hoped to find his birth parents, dozens of people in South Korea stepped forward, claiming to be his birth parents. DNA testing confirmed that a man named Kim Jae-su was Toby's biological father. The two were reunited February 27, 2007, in South Korea. After many hugs and tears, Toby discovered something unexpected and wonderful—he also had a younger brother. On that momentous day Toby was finally able to ask why he ended up in an orphanage. Kim Jae-su explained that Toby's mother lost him while shopping at an outdoor market in the city of Busan. The family searched for him and checked local orphanages as well. The police took Toby to an orphanage a long distance from where his family lived, so Kim Jae-su and his wife never found him.[12]

Prior to meeting his father, Toby had some exposure to his Korean heritage. When he was young, Toby attended a Korean Heritage Camp for a few days during several summers. The purpose of the camp is to help children who are born in Korea and adopted in the United States find out more about their native culture. Campers learn Korean history, cook some Korean dishes, do calligraphy, and enjoy Korean sports such as Tae-kwon-do. As an adult, Toby worked at a Korean Heritage Camp as a counselor. He helped kids learn about their Korean culture and also shared his struggles of being in the minority, as well as other adoption-related issues.[13]

What about You?

Do you wonder about your birth parents and why they placed you? Are you curious about what your life would have been like if you had been raised in your birth country? Would you like to investigate your heritage and birth culture? Don't be afraid to ask your parents for help. Search for a local group of adoptees from your birth country. Think about planning your own trip so you can experience your culture for yourself. If you find that questions about your background keep popping up, then make the time to search for the answers you want to know. Learn what makes you unique and special. Seek, learn, and connect. Celebrate your heritage and who you are.

On November 2, 2006, The International Adoptee Congress (IAC) met for the first time in Washington, D.C. This organization is made up of internationally adopted persons. The members of the IAC hope to empower and support international adoptees. They also support adoption groups and work with adoptive families, adoption agencies, and adoption professionals to help create healthy adoptive families.

During its first meeting in 2006, this organization discussed ways to empower adoptees, considered ways they can work within the adoption community, evaluated resources available to adoptees and ways to improve and promote these resources, and launched a national agenda that all adoptees can participate in. You can find out more about the International Adoptee Congress or become a member at www.internationaladopteecongress.org.[14]

Discussion Questions

Have you done any research on your birth heritage?

In what ways to you feel unique or different because of your heritage? How do those feelings affect you?

Do you think internationally adopted teens face certain issues other adopted teens don't face? If so, how do you work through those issues?

What advice would you give to other teens born in another country and adopted in the United States?

How can being "different" be a good thing sometimes?

Notes

1. Ben, e-mail correspondence, February 21, 2006.
2. Adopting.org, "China Eases One-Child Policy," www.adopting.org/adoptions/china-eases-one-child-policy.html (accessed July 18, 2006) and "Family Planning," www.adopting.org/uni/frame.php?url=cnn.com/interactive/specials/9908/china.social.overview/content/family.planning.html (accessed July 18, 2006).
3. Hollee McGinnis, e-mail correspondence, December 5, 2006.

4. Kelly-Anne Suarez, "Role Emerges for Actress as Real Princess," *Chicago Tribune*, September 17, 2006, 18.

5. *The Adoption History Project*, "Proxy Adoptions," www.uoregon.edu/~adoption/topics/proxy.htm (accessed September 1, 2006).

6. *The Adoption History Project*, "Adoption Statistics," www.uoregon.edu/~adoption/topics/adoptionstatistics.htm (accessed August 24, 2006).

7. U.S. Department of State, "Immigrant Visas Issued to Orphans Coming to the U.S.," travel.state.gov/family/adoption/stats/stats_451.html (accessed April 13, 2007).

8. Michael, e-mail correspondence, March 29, 2006.

9. "College Course on the Adoptee Experience," *Adoptive Families* (June 2006), 11.

10. Katy Robinson, *A Single Square Picture* (New York: Berkeley, 2002), 10.

11. Adoptive Families, "Adoption Events," www.adoptivefamilies.com/calendar (accessed March 7, 2006).

12. Burt Herman, "Olympic Skier Toby Dawson Reunites with Korean Family," *USA Today Online*, February 27, 2007, www.usatoday.com/sports/olympics/winter/2007-02-28-dawson-father_x.htm (accessed April 9, 2007).

13. *Toby Dawson Biography*, www.nbcolympics.com/athletes/5058549/detail.html (accessed February 25, 2006).

14. International Adoptee Congress, www.internationaladopteecongress.org (accessed September 13, 2006).

TRANSRACIAL ADOPTION

···

"I know I am different from my friends. I know I have had to deal with different things because my parents are white and I am black. I am not like other black kids, I didn't have black parents. I wasn't raised in that culture, but I don't really feel different for it. I have parents just like everyone else, parents that love me and support me and guide me, like I hope everyone else has."[1]—Alanna, age 18

Teens adopted transracially will have many different experiences at home and with friends—some will be encouraging, positive, inclusive, and affirming, and others will not. This chapter will focus on how various teens choose to recognize their cultural backgrounds, celebrate their differences, and deal with difficulties. Hopefully, you will gain some insights and new ideas that will prove helpful for you.

Race: An Issue for Some

As a teen who was adopted transracially, you may find it difficult if you don't share many physical characteristics with the other members of your family. Perhaps the family photos hanging in your house serve as a constant reminder that you look different from your siblings and parents. You may never hear that you have your mother's eyes or your father's hair, as is often said of your parents' biological children. It might seem as if your appearance continually alerts everyone you meet that you are different—like a sign posted on your forehead announcing to strangers you are adopted. And sometimes you might just get tired of being different, and tired of explaining your situation.

> **! It's a Fact**
>
> A transracial adoption occurs when a family of one race adopts a child or children who belong to a different race.

Most families that adopt a child of another race usually belong to the dominant racial group,[2] and in the United States that race is Caucasian.[3] More often than not, adults choose to live in a neighborhood or town that is predominantly the same race that they are. So for most transracially adopted teens, this means that they are a minority in their family, school, and community.

Patricia, a Caucasian woman who adopted two African American children, shares a discussion she had with friends as she and her husband were deciding the best place to raise their family. "We asked our black friends where we should live when we adopted our kids, and they said, 'Stay in your neighborhood because it has the best schools and safest streets. The kids will get the culture later, but they can never make up for a poor education.'"[4]

The United States is a rather diverse nation where people enjoy many freedoms and opportunities that are not found in most other countries in the world. But real-life experiences remind us that race and appearance often become a determining factor, whether blatantly or in a more subtle manner, that causes people of minority races to face prejudice. So your feelings of "being different" may be compounded by the way others react to you as well.

Race: Not an Issue for Others

While race is often an issue for many transracially adopted teens, it isn't necessarily a major problem for all. Some teens are fortunate and find a group of friends who look past skin color or race and focus on their similarities and building friendships. Liana, a seventeen-year-old who was adopted from Guatemala and now lives near Chicago, finds her school and classmates are generally very accepting and inclusive.

Liana shares her experiences:[5]

The majority of my friends are Caucasian, but that doesn't bother me. I wasn't raised to view people of different races as different. My parents have shown me how to accept everyone the same. Color has had no effect on me, although now and then I have friends who are curious as to why my mom is Caucasian and I'm not. My father passed away when I was a

Liana (right), and one of her friends, Kristen

freshman (he was Caucasian as well), and now perhaps some people use their imagination and think I am a "mix" between Caucasian and black, but I'm not. Even though a majority of my friends are white, I have quite a few who are Spanish. What's the difference between friendships that are Caucasian with black, or Caucasian with Spanish, or Spanish with black? To me, there really is no difference, and it's the same way in my family.

The school I attend is very diverse. There are many races in my school—Middle Eastern, Asian, Spanish, white, and black. Our school is very open to kids with different backgrounds. We don't exclude any group, which allows students to become friends with a variety of people, not just all one background. Just because most of my friends are Caucasian doesn't mean we don't do the same things as teenagers of any race. I don't act different with my Spanish friends than I do with my Caucasian friends. We drive around, go to movies, go out to dinner, or just have fun watching a TV show at one of our houses. I don't see race or color affecting the kids in the

It's a Fact

In 2008, U.S. citizens adopted 17,416 children from foreign countries (13 percent of total adoptions that year).[6]

town where I live, and I'm thankful for that. People here always have open arms to everyone.

Keeping Up Appearances

People all over the world place a great deal of emphasis on appearance. This fact is evident in many cultures. Although there are very specific stereotypes and expectations of beauty in America, other countries are not immune to this type of thinking. And sometimes the quest for characteristics that are deemed "desirable" among certain people leads to drastic measures. For example, foot binding was a common practice of women in East Asia for years, which created useless, yet very coveted, small feet. People in certain parts of Africa have a history of neck elongation, accomplished by wearing many rings around their neck. The list of examples could go on and on, but the lesson here is clear. At the very root of human nature is the importance of appearance and the belief that a person should look a certain way, whatever that happens to be for a particular society, to fit in, so he or she wouldn't be viewed as or treated differently.

As a teen, you are well aware that wearing clothes with a certain label conveys a certain status. You know that having the latest hairstyle or a popular logo on a pair of shoes can be key to fitting in with the cool crowd at school. So it's easy to understand why teens may feel out of place when the majority of kids they hang out with look different from them. As a result, transracial adoptions may have more complicated issues than same-race adoptions. Teens adopted transracially must deal with the visual and cultural differences among their family members and their peers. As you learn the ways you can cope with these differences, it's important to remember that they are just that—differences.

Many people today act as if appearance and race don't matter a great deal. They want to believe that, in this modern day, the world has finally become "color-blind" and that everyone is viewed the same or equal. In fact, it can be "politically incorrect" to acknowledge that race is important. But reality tells us that race does matter.

Lessons at Lunch

The town of Berkeley, located in northern California, has people of many races. The residents who live there like it that way. They are proud of their cultural diversity. There is only one public high school in Berkeley. It is comprised of a very diverse student population and also boasts above-average SAT scores.

In a school made up of students of many races and nationalities, it's interesting to observe what occurs at Berkeley High School over the lunch hour. If you

"Why do I hear people say that America is a free country with an abundance of opportunities? Based on my experiences and the stories I hear from other black teens, these are not in any way, shape, or form given to all peoples in this country."[8]—Sasha, age 19

were to visit this school's cafeteria, the first thing you might notice is how the students group together by race. Asian kids are usually sitting together in a group. Likewise, the African American students will be in another area, Caucasians in yet another section, and the Latinos together at their table. The students seek out and tend to socialize mostly with others of their own race or background. It is surprising to note this self-segregation in a town that celebrates its diversity. The same trend can be observed in most high schools all over the country—students from the same racial group tend to flock together. This highlights the fact that although people of different races or cultures may be placed together in certain situations, they tend to gravitate toward those that are most like them.[7]

Rising above the Norm

The question transracially adopted teens, and society as a whole, must ask themselves is: Why do people generally feel more comfortable with others who are like them, while they tend to segregate themselves from those who are different? Is it out of fear? Ignorance? Is it due to the socialization process, whereby people learn to perceive what is "normal" or "acceptable?"

Perhaps an even bigger question a teen should ask is, "Do I want to settle for this natural human tendency or attempt to change it?" When people magnify the differences between them, this can produce destructive behavior that leads to discrimination, misunderstandings, and even hate. As a transracially adopted teen, you can try to focus on the sameness in people and look for the ways in which everyone is similar, which could bring powerful changes in your life. This

A Fact You Should Know

The genome, which is all of the DNA material in the cells of living organisms,[9] is 99.9 percent the same in all people.[10] Although people of many races may look very different on the outside, they are actually only 0.1 percent different on the inside.

type of thinking leads to inclusion, understanding, and love. You can strive for a healthy balance in your life, where you feel comfortable reaching out and developing friendships with those of different races, while still enjoying the friendship of others in your own race. It's important to recognize and celebrate your own heritage and the qualities that make you unique and special, as you appreciate the similarities you share with others.

Same on the Inside—Different on the Outside

Transracially adopted teens, whether they are born in the United States or adopted internationally, often share some of the same concerns. One issue many

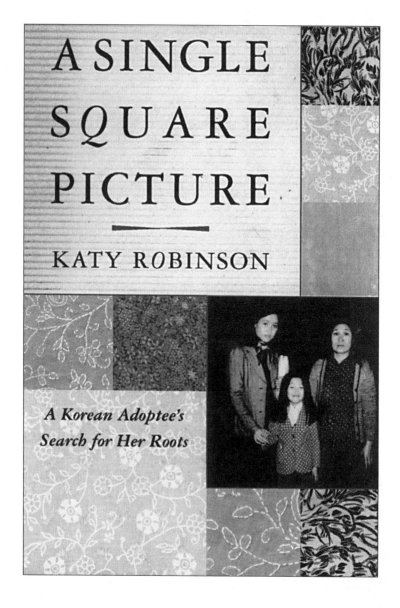

A SINGLE SQUARE PICTURE

KATY ROBINSON

A Korean Adoptee's Search for Her Roots

face is the feeling that people misinterpret who they truly are, or what lies on the inside, based on how they appear on the outside.

Katy Robinson, a woman who was born in Korea and later adopted by a family in the United States, shares her experiences in a book she wrote, titled *A Single Square Picture*. Katy explains how she felt American inside, just like her friends and family, but on the outside she felt as though she was wearing a different shell from those around her.

Katy's adoption journey began when she was seven and her unmarried mother placed her in an orphanage. Katy's mother made this painful decision out of love and concern for Katy's future. She wanted her daughter to get a good education and have the many opportunities an American family could provide. Her wish came true when Katy was adopted by a couple from Utah who had three biological sons. Katy and her adoptive family lived in Salt Lake City, a town with little cultural diversity. In fact, she was the only Asian child at her school. In her book, Katy describes the conflicts she dealt with—from those around her and within herself as a transracially adopted teen.

A Single Square Picture shares Katy's joys and frustrations during her adjustment to life in America and her longing to return to Korea in the early days. As time progressed, Katy lost her ability to speak, read, or write in Korean. It wasn't long before she forgot about her favorite Korean dishes and other Korean ways, too. The author reflects on how quickly it seemed as if she had always been in America.

In her twenties Katy felt a need to connect with her roots and heritage. She decided to search for her birth parents in Korea. She initially traveled to Korea for a short four-day visit but returned later and lived there for a year. Her book tells the fascinating tale of her search and eventual reunion with several members of her birth family. After spending a significant amount of time with her biological family members, Katy began to more fully realize the extent of their cultural differences. This is a well-written, powerful story of growing, searching, learning, and healing.

Katy Robinson holding a photo of herself taken at age one while she was still in Korea. Katy was given the Korean name "Kim Ji-yun" when she was born.

Katy and her biological father, whom she fondly calls "Appa," while they were visiting a park in Seoul in June 2006.

Katy shares her feelings when she was young:

Growing up, I didn't know a single other person who had been adopted. That, added to the fact I was the only Asian in my school, home, and community, made me feel isolated and alone. I hid my discomfort by trying to be the all-American girl and totally denying my Korean heritage. I didn't want to talk about being adopted; I just wanted to fit in. It wasn't until much later, at the age of twenty-seven, that I became curious about my birth family and country. Today, I realize how lucky I am to have such a rich blend of cultures and a loving family on both sides of the Pacific.[11]

Knowledge Is Power

Sasha, a nineteen-year-old adopted teen, grew up in an adoptive family comprised of several races. As a young child, Sasha struggled with his appearance and racial identity. He was constantly reminded that he was different from his family by questions from outsiders. Sasha explains:

I've been raised in an interracial family my whole life. My parents and my older brother (their biological child) being white, my younger brother be-

Most of the children adopted in the United States (under the age of eighteen) were born in Asia. The 2000 U.S. Census revealed that a total of 123,000 children who were adopted from Asia are now living in the United States. Korea had the largest number of children, around 57,000, that were adopted into the United States. Of those 57,000 children, about 48,000 were under eighteen when the study was conducted in 2000.[12]

ing half-Latino and half-black, and me, half-black and half-Indian. Family pictures tell a million tales of what it's like to be in a family where difference is obvious, and my identity is in question—by everyone who wonders why the little brown child is with a white family.

But for all the pieces and parts that make up my whole, I know I must own them all. Studying and writing has helped me fathom those pieces, question those pieces, and understand why they are so important. I may not be any closer to putting a definition to them, but the feelings and experiences are there, waiting to be made sense of and desperately seeking analysis.[13]

As the years passed, Sasha needed to find a way to resolve these racial issues and gain a fuller understanding of his identity. Being of mixed race, Sasha felt his situation was more complex that that of other teens in an interracial family. Over time, Sasha discovered that the color of his skin dictated the way many people viewed him.

Sasha hoped to find answers to some of his deepest questions by learning more about human cultures and identities through studies at college. He decided to attend Hampshire College, a progressive school in Amherst, Massachusetts, where students can formulate their own concentrated study. Sasha started out studying photojournalism at college until he learned about the field of ethnology. Then he decided to focus on ethnography, sociology, and photography. Using these three areas, Sasha has been able to study the construction of identities through the image/visual, as well as the ways this affects people's actions. Using memoir and ethnographic writing as tools to tell his story and that of others, Sasha has explored issues of authenticity, identity complexity, and political identity.

After completing his first year at college, Sasha was very excited about what he had learned. "As I continually move and shake within my work, I reach epiphany after epiphany, wondering if there will ever be an end to the eye-opening

Ethnography is one branch, or part, of anthropology—a term you may be familiar with. Anthropology is the scientific study of the origin, the behavior, and the physical, social, and cultural development of humans. Ethnography is defined as the part of cultural anthropology that focuses specifically on the study of human cultures.[14]

Ethnography isn't always specifically scientific. At the college Sasha attends, ethnography is approached from the point of view of art and cultural preservation and as a descriptive rather than an analytic endeavor.

change that occurs when you use ethnography to explore anything. The most valuable tool I've received out of an entire career of education is the ability to take apart my world and reassemble it again—questioning and thinking, reflecting and wondering—the process is endless." For Sasha, being able to spend time and energy focusing on issues of race and identity has been crucial for his personal growth. Choosing this path of study in college has been very meaningful and has allowed him to develop life-changing ideas and beliefs.

Choosing the Right Paths

While this academic path has been very helpful for Sasha, you don't need a degree in ethnography to gain a better sense of your racial identity. You can learn more about your racial heritage from support groups or heritage camps. Try joining a discussion group or start one of your own. Check out books on this topic from your library. You can seek out events and opportunities that will help further develop your sense of personal identity. You can also learn from hearing about other transracially adopted teens' experiences. To that end, Sasha shares how his perceptions and ideas about race have changed through the years:

When I was younger I had a lot of resentment about my identity. Reflecting, reading books like Toni Morrison's *The Bluest Eye*, there was a time when I wanted to be white. To be able to dress up as my heroes on Halloween, to be able to look like the neighbors I had and the friends I made, the people that were on TV and teaching me in classrooms; I realize now that a lot of what I was feeling was set up that way, institutionally embedded. Systems of oppression which as a child I could have never understood.

What kid could realize that the reason they get depressed about dressing up for Halloween was actually because images in popular culture have been embedded to disengage healthy strong people of color? I just thought Batman didn't look good black. It was a lot bigger than all of that, and I'm thankful to be able to do work and explore issues of identity now. I think back to high school, a miserable place for most people, and it was stifling, conforming, and unproductive. The work I've been able to do in college has saved my personal identity.[13]

Looking for Something New

The story of a seventeen-year-old girl named McKenzie Forbes, who was adopted from China when she was two, appeared March 23, 2006, in a *New York Times* article. In that article, McKenzie shared that she feels different from other teenagers at times because of her cultural background and appearance. She also acknowledges that she feels a special bond with many Asian teens she meets.

When McKenzie began to think about college, she did some research to find universities that had Asian student groups on campus. She decided to apply only to colleges that had Asian groups. McKenzie looked forward to meeting and spending time with other Asian students. While McKenzie was certainly not ostracizing herself from social gatherings of non-Asian students, she simply found that spending some time with other Asian teens was a helpful and affirming activity for her.

In the 1970s, several cultural groups and organizations discouraged transracial adoptions. They believed transracially adopted children lost access to their culture and heritage, and some groups went so far as to call these adoptions "cultural genocide." Certain adoption agencies during this time would not allow a couple of one race to adopt a child of another race.

Recent data shows that an increasing number of families are adopting transracially. For example, almost all of the 26 percent of black children in foster care who were adopted in 2004 found homes with a white family. This represents a nearly 14 percent increase from 1998 in white couples adopting black children. One reason for this surge in transracial adoptions may be due to a revised federal law that states that adoption agencies that receive funding from the government can no longer stop parents from adopting a child based on race.[15]

> ### ! It's a Fact
>
> China's one-child policy, which strongly encourages each family to have only one child, caused thousands of Chinese women to place their babies in orphanages. China changed its adoption laws in 1991, making these children available for people in other countries to adopt. Since 1991, families in the United States have adopted over 72,000 children from China.[16]

Bonded by Common Experiences

The *Times* article also described the experiences of another girl adopted from China named Qiu Meng Fogarty. Sixteen-year-old Qiu Meng likes to remember her heritage and has several Chinese pictures hanging up in her bedroom. Qiu Meng has two close friends, Hope and Celena, who were also adopted from China when they were young. The girls have been friends for years. Qiu Meng believes the friendship has lasted so long because the girls share the same Chinese heritage. They also can relate to each other's adoption situation. Qui Meng, Hope, and Celena attended a summer camp for adopted children together. Their special time at camp was yet another common experience that helped to bond the three friends. Qui Meng keeps special reminders of her heritage in her room and has also found value in seeking out special events, such as the summer camp for adopted children, where she can learn more about her heritage and meet new Asian friends.[16]

Teens Ask

Katrina Carlisle, a social worker who has spent seventeen years in the field of adoption, answered questions from internationally adopted teens in chapter 8, and also tackles some of the issues that kids adopted transracially face in this chapter. Ms. Carlisle draws on her many years as a birth family search specialist and her personal experiences as an adoptive mother. Her son was born in Korea.

There are times I wish I looked more like my family and my friends. How can I deal with those feelings?

First of all, let me say you are not alone. Many young people wish they looked like their friends, even if they aren't racially different. Those that are overweight

Unfortunately, not every adopted person knows his or her racial or ethnic heritage. Some people go through life looking in a mirror, hoping to find clues about their ethnicity. One woman, Debra Anne Royer, was adopted at birth and had no information about her birth parents. For years she wondered what race or races were in her background. Some friends guessed Cambodian, while others speculated Iranian because of Debra's darker skin and wide nose. When DNA testing began making the news, Debra decided to use this technological breakthrough to find some answers. She paid $200 for the testing. Debra provided a sample of her DNA from a swab on the inside of her cheek, and modern science gave her the information she longed for. The results showed that ancestors on her mother's side were most likely Native American. Debra was thrilled to finally discover some pieces of her ethnic background.[17]

wish they were thin, those that are thin wish they were muscular, those with curly hair wish they had straight, and on and on and on. When you are racially different than your friends, it causes an even greater feeling of not fitting in.

You can always wear the same kind of clothes and participate in the same activities as your friends, but nothing can change your skin color or facial features. So the best thing you can do is to learn to embrace who you are. Learn more about your birth culture, seek out opportunities to interact with others that look like you, read magazines with photos of people like you, and so on. As you learn to appreciate and love your heritage, you will begin to appreciate how your appearance reflects that heritage.

Keep in mind, your friends chose to have a relationship with you. Obviously they are comfortable with the way you look. As you are agonizing about your differences, they may be envying your skin tone or other features. Find a friend to share your feelings with; maybe you can help each other deal with feelings of insecurity.

Finally, it is always good to share your feelings with your parents or a school counselor. Let someone know if you feel you could benefit from some additional counseling.

Sometimes people ask questions about why I look different from my parents and it makes me angry. What answer can I give them that will make me feel better?

Movie: *Remember the Titans*

Remember the Titans (2000) is a movie based on a true story of how one town triumphed over prejudice to win a state football championship, and more importantly, create peace and understanding in the community. Set in Alexandria, Virginia, the movie takes place in 1971, during one of the peaks of racial tension in America. Oscar-winning actor Denzel Washington played the role of Coach Boone, the new football coach at T.C. Williams High School. After replacing the successful former white coach, he was met with anger and hostility from the players and their families. Boone was faced with the seemingly impossible task of finding a way to unite a team, and a town, divided by race. During summer football training camp, Coach Boone required each boy to interview every player of a different race on the team and learn about their families and lives. The racial walls soon began to break down as the boys forged meaningful and lasting friendships. This story confronts an issue that many Americans still struggle with today in a touching and very real way.

I can't say what answer might make you feel better, as each of us is different. But there are a variety of approaches you can take. If you feel like educating the other person, you can say something like, "My family was built by adoption," or "I joined my family through adoption." If you want to go into greater detail, you can tell what my son always calls the "story." His story starts like this, "I was born in South Korea and traveled to the United States at the age of six months . . ." You can share whatever details you choose in your story.

There may be times when you prefer not to answer personal questions. This is understandable for many reasons. In this situation you might try saying, "Oh, it's a long story and I don't have time to go into it right now." Humor is always good. You could look shocked and say, "You don't think I look like my parents?" If someone is really getting on your nerves, you can respond, "That's really personal, why do you need to know?"

You may choose to use different responses at different times, or you can find one you like and stick with it. Just do what feels comfortable to you. You are not obligated to share your personal information with anyone.

> **! Something to Think About**
>
> Have you ever longed to have a family member that shared some of your physical characteristics? Would you like to be able to compare your nose, mouth, or ears with those belonging to your siblings or parents? While you may not have the same features as your current family members, you might in the future. If you have children someday, you may finally have a little face that mirrors your own. You will be part of a brand-new family that shares your genes and possibly many aspects of your appearance.

The Changing Face of America

For teens who feel somewhat out of place because they are a minority, it might be helpful to know that diversity is on the rise. While the United States is currently comprised of mostly white, non–Hispanic people, the 2000 Census report indicated that the United States is becoming more diverse. It cites immigration and higher birth rates among minority groups than whites as the two main causes for this shift in demographics. The Census Bureau also predicts this trend will continue.

Also, the number of international adoptions is increasing, and families comprised of different races are becoming more and more common. The U.S. Department of State immigration visa records reflect some of the many countries of origin for children adopted into the United States. The following list of twenty-seven countries is compiled from these records between 2000 and 2005: Azerbaijan, Belarus, Brazil, Bulgaria, Cambodia, China, Colombia, Ethiopia, Guatemala, Haiti, India, Jamaica, Kazakhstan, Korea, Liberia, Mexico, Moldova, Nepal, Nigeria, Peru, Philippines, Poland, Romania, Russia, Thailand, Ukraine, and Vietnam.[18] As adoption continually changes the makeup of U.S. families, society's view of how a family should look is also slowly changing.

Race and Family

One example of how people's beliefs about race and family have changed through the years is the story of Lynette Cole. Lynette was ten months old and living in a foster care home in 1978 when Gail and Larry Cole decided to adopt her. At that time, the courts in Michigan, where the Coles lived, would not allow them to

Increase in Minority Population–Predictions from the Census Bureau

Year	White (non-Hispanic)	All Other Races
2000	69.1%	30.9%
2005	67.1%	32.9%
2010	64.8%	35.2%
2015	62.8%	37.2%
2020	60.8%	39.2%[19]

adopt Lynette because she was part Puerto Rican and part Caucasian. Michigan law stated that a couple of one race could not adopt a child of a different race, and the Coles were Caucasian. Determined to adopt Lynette, Gail and Larry Cole both quit their jobs and moved to another state where they could adopt Lynette regardless of her race.

Lynette Cole thrived in her loving adoptive home, although some of her teachers reported that she was a slow learner. In the year 2000, Lynette won the title of Miss Tennessee. She went on to be crowned Miss USA in the 2000 pageant. In 2001, Lynette began to help work on adoption issues with the staff of the Congressional Coalition on Adoption. She hopes her adoption experiences and knowledge will benefit others.[20]

Fortunately, ideas about family and adoption have changed drastically from the 1970s. Today a child of any race or nationality can be adopted by a family in any state (as long as the adoptive family completes a home study and meets certain state requirements). As you grow and learn from your own experiences of living in an interracial family, you may discover ways you can use your experiences to help others and bring about more change in the future.

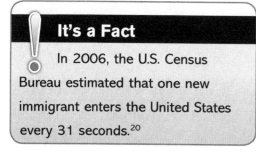

It's a Fact

In 2006, the U.S. Census Bureau estimated that one new immigrant enters the United States every 31 seconds.[20]

If Things Get Really Rough

Teens adopted transracially face a variety of issues and problems, depending on their personal situation. These racial issues can be worked through in various ways and with the help of many different people. Parents, support groups, books, classes, heritage camps, and talking with others can help teens overcome problems that may seem almost overwhelming at times.

Counseling is another option that teens with more serious or ongoing issues should consider. It may be time to seek a counselor if you exhibit symptoms such as depression, withdrawing from social gatherings, hopelessness, or any other unusual thoughts or behavior that lasts for a long time. A trained counselor can offer insights and ideas that friends and family cannot. Everyone has good and bad days, but be sure to ask someone you trust for help when you need it.

What about You?

So how can you deal with the problems you face as a transracially adopted teen? Perhaps spending time with other teens who share your cultural background or adoption experience would help create healthy and affirming friendships, like it did for McKenzie and Qui Meng. You might even consider starting your own local group for transracially adopted teens. Katy Robinson found answers to many of her racial issues when she learned about the Korean culture during her stay in Korea and met several members of her birth family. If you were adopted from another country, perhaps an opportunity like this will open up to you.

College courses helped Sasha gain a better understanding of race and his identity. Check out what classes are available at your school or local college. Katrina Carlisle pointed out that something as simple as being prepared for annoying questions from outsiders can protect you from suddenly being taken off guard. Do you have answers ready for the questions you are often asked? Ms. Carlisle also made the helpful observation that most teens tend to place themselves under a microscope and find every tiny thing they see that makes them "different" from others. Often, teens focus so much on these small differences that they begin to believe that these make them unacceptable. What are you focusing on? Are you overly conscious about certain aspects of your appearance? Try talking to a trusted friend or parent about your concerns. Realize that all teens, including those of every race, adopted or not, face doubts about how they look and experience times when they don't feel like they fit in.

Put It in Writing

A simple exercise that might help you work through your feelings of not fitting in is to get out a pen and paper and make a few lists. On the first list, write down all the things you have in common with the members of your family. Think of the same foods, sports, activities, etc., that you all like. What are your common dislikes or fears? Then make another list of similarities you share with your friends. As you look at these lists, you may realize that you are not as different from others as you thought. Now make one more list. This time write down all the things that make you unique. What qualities, talents, interests, and features make you *you*? Do you play an instrument? Can you rattle off all the baseball statistics of the major league players? Do you have beautiful, distinctive eyes or shiny, thick hair that your friends envy? Taking stock of what you have in common with others, and the attributes that make you special, may give you confidence and a healthy self-esteem that will help you feel comfortable in groups of many races and cultural backgrounds.

This Won't Happen Overnight

Finding your identity and how you uniquely fit in your family, school, and community takes time. You are slowly growing in your self-awareness and understanding of who you are. Maturing and developing a healthy racial identity is a process.

As you discover new ideas about yourself and your personal identity, try to focus on the progress you have made rather than the obstacles that still stand in your way. If you have a bad day or a rough week—don't give up. Keep searching and looking for others who you can relate to. Keep striving to learn and grow. Enjoy who you are and who you are becoming as you travel on your life journey.

Discussion Questions

Do you think a person's outward appearance tells a lot about what the person is like on the inside? Why?

What are some things you have in common with your family members?

What do you wish your family could really get, or understand, about you? How could you let them know that?

What is the most difficult challenge you face as a member of a transracial family?

Notes

1. Alanna, e-mail correspondence, March 10, 2006.
2. Lois Melina, "How Do We Define Belonging?" www.adoptivefamilies.com/articles.php?aid= 611 (accessed August 25, 2006).

3. U.S. Census Bureau, 2000 Brief, "Overview of Race and Hispanic Origin," p. 3, www.census.gov/prod/2001pubs/c2kbr01-1.pdf (accessed August 25, 2006).

4. Patricia Evans, e-mail correspondence, December 21, 2006.

5. Liana, e-mail correspondence, August 28, 2006.

6. Child Welfare Information Gateway, "How Many Children Were Adopted in 2007 and 2008? Number and Trends," 2011, www.childwelfare.gov/pubs/adopted0708.pdf#Page=26&view=Fit (accessed March 29, 2012).

7. Gail Steinberg and Beth Hall, *Inside Transracial Adoption* (Indianapolis: Perspectives, 2000), 61.

8. Sasha, e-mail correspondence, July 24, 2006.

9. National Human Genome Research Institute, "Talking Glossary," www.genome.gov/glossary.cfm?key=genome (accessed August 25, 2006).

10. Human Genome Project Sequence Analysis, "Insights Learned from the Sequence," www.ornl.gov/hgmis/project/journals/insights.html (accessed August 25, 2006).

11. Katy Robinson, e-mail correspondence, August 17, 2006.

12. U.S. Census Bureau, "Adopted Children of the Householder by Place of Birth and Age: 2000," www.census.gov/prod/2003pubs/censr-6.pdf (accessed February 28, 2006).

13. Sasha, e-mail correspondence, March 4, 2006.

14. *The American Heritage Dictionary of the English Language*, 4th ed. (New York: Houghton Mifflin, 2000).

15. Family Research Council, "Breaking Down Barriers to Adoption," www.frc.org/get.cfm?i=WU06H14 (accessed August 28, 2006).

16. U.S. Department of State, "Significant Source Countries of Immigrant Orphans (Totals of IR–3 and IR–4 Immigrant Visas Issued to Orphans) Fiscal Years 1992–2011," www.travel.state.gov/pdf/MultiYearTableXIII.pdf (accessed September 19, 2012).

17. Claudia Kalb, "In Our Blood," *Newsweek*, February 6, 2006, 47.

18. U.S. Department of State, "Immigrant Visas Issued to Orphans Coming to the U.S." travel.state.gov/family/adoption/stats/stats_451.html (accessed August 17, 2006).

19. U.S. Department of Health and Human Services, "Changing Demographics and the Implications for Physicians, Nurses, and Other Health Workers," bhpr.hrsa.gov/healthworkforce/reports/changedemo/composition.htm#3.1 (accessed August 25, 2006).

20. Wikipedia, "Lynette Cole," en.wikipedia.org/wiki/Lynnette_Cole (accessed August 17, 2006); Adoption Clubhouse, "Interesting People," www.adoptionclubhouse.org/02_people/05_interesting/01_interesting.html (accessed February 28, 2006); Mary Landrieu, "Miss USA 2000 Joins Adoption Coalition Staff," www.senate.gov/~landrieu/releases/01/2001321B12.html (accessed February 28, 2006).

21. "U.S. Population Passes 300 Million Mark," www.boston.com/news/nation/washington/articles/2006/10/17/us_population_passes_300_million_mark/ (accessed October 26, 2006).

ADOPTED AT AN OLDER AGE

"I know she didn't want to give me up, but I know she didn't want me to die. My other brother died of starvation. I suppose that's why she had to give me up for adoption."[1]—Emily, age 17

Not all adopted children are placed in their adoptive homes when they are babies, or even when they are very young. A great number of children are adopted at older ages. This type of adoption situation occurs for a number of reasons.

In some countries, extremely overcrowded living conditions, severe poverty, a critical food shortage, war, or other serious or sudden dangers can cause birth parents to relinquish their child to an adoption agency or an orphanage with the hopes that he or she will have a better future. Parents in these types of situations make this difficult decision to save their child's life. In certain instances, a serious or terminal illness can lead to placement. Sometimes the death of one or both parents necessitates adoption if there are no family members who are willing or capable of raising the children left behind.

Sometimes a child may be placed for adoption against the wishes of his or her birth parents. If a child is not properly taken care of, abused, or in danger, then state authorities may intervene and place that child in foster care while seeking a permanent family though adoption. Because authorities are reluctant to terminate parental rights before allowing time for the parents to improve their situation, and because the legal process can be quite slow, children often stay in foster care many years before being adopted as an "older" child. This type of an adoption can become extremely emotional and require outside help such as counselors to help a child work through issues with past abuse and adapt to a new family and life.

A New Beginning

An adopted child's new home might be very close to where he or she grew up. It may be a grandparent's house across town or a new family in a nearby city. However, sometimes an adopted child ends up moving far away. Their adoptive family may be in another state or a country thousands of miles across the ocean. Moving is a major adjustment for any child but is especially difficult for children moving to a new country. In addition to fitting into a new family, these children may also need to learn a new language and how to live in a new culture. More detailed information on how adopted children can cope with these changes can be found in chapters 8 and 9.

Lack of Nurturing

An older child faces different hurdles than children who are adopted when they are babies or infants. Older adoptees may spend several months or even years in foster homes, orphanages, or group homes before being adopted. Because of the sheer number of children waiting to be adopted in these types of living situations, individual children don't have the luxury of spending a great deal of time with a nurturing, caring adult. Without the proper love and affirmation from adults, a child's self-esteem and ability to interact socially can be significantly affected. Their cognitive functioning may also be delayed. Researchers who reviewed twenty-nine studies of children who had lived in orphanages in Russia, Romania, and China concluded that there was a significant link between the amount of time a child lived in an orphanage and later ongoing problems. Studies indicate that children who remain in group care for more that a year have a greater chance of developing behavioral problems or exhibiting a cognitive delay. These issues can later cause a child to have difficulties in school.[2]

Loss of Birth Parents

Nearly all children form strong bonds with their parents during their formative years. Most children experience tremendous grief and personal loss when they are separated from the birth parents who have raised them. Many teens who are adopted when they are older must overcome the loss of their birth parents.

Emily, an adopted teen from Cambodia, first faced her father's death, and then the loss of her mother and siblings when she left Cambodia. After being placed with an adoptive family in the United States in 1999, Emily began the process of learning how to move past her grief and anger as she looks toward a better future.

A Very Real Reality Show

A local cable channel in New York regularly airs a television show that features teens waiting to be adopted.
These teens tell their stories of loneliness, rejection, and
pain as they continue to hold out hope that they will find a family to call their own.
The hard reality is that in December 2005, there were around 17,000 kids currently living in foster homes under New York's welfare system. About half of these
children waiting to find a permanent home were teenagers. The city has been fighting hard to find adoptive families for teens. It wants to dispel the common belief
that teens in foster care are too difficult and troubled to adopt.

Marie, a seventeen-year-old girl who appeared on a show aired in 2005, shared
her thoughts with the audience about the fifteen years she had spent in various
foster homes. Marie still hopes to find a family of her own before she leaves the
foster care system when she reaches the maximum age of eighteen.[3]

(c) C Papile 1998

Emily's Story

Growing up in Cambodia, Emily was one of four children in her family. She had an older sister and two younger brothers. Although Emily's family did not have a lot, they all worked together and made ends meet. When Emily's father died, things suddenly changed. The family soon became very poor and homeless. Three months after her father passed away, Emily's mother decided to place Emily and her youngest brother up for adoption. Emily doesn't know how old she was when she was adopted (and isn't sure of her actual age today), but believes she was between the ages of eight and ten when she joined her adoptive family.

Although Emily has lived in the United States with her caring adoptive family for many years, she still struggles with the decision her mother made. She misses her family, culture, and homeland, and often wonders why her life had to turn out as it did. She is hurt and confused about why her mother chose to place her in another home through adoption. Emily recently wrote her birth mother a letter and shared her thoughts about her adoption. Although writing the letter brought back many feelings she had been trying to suppress, putting her anger and frustration into words on paper also helped Emily begin a healing process. Emily shares her thoughts:

> Why did she give me up? I understand that my mom had to give some of us up, but why were my brother and I the ones? It just feels like she didn't love me as much as my other siblings—like my brother and I were the least loved. I guess maybe we were just unlucky. I have so many feelings. I still miss my mom, but I'm also mad at my mom for giving me up. I know she tried to keep me, but I think we could have worked something out. If my mom would have talked to me about her reasons before I left, I might understand.

While Emily worked hard to adjust to life in the United States, she also worried about her brother. "What also makes me so miserable is being separated from my brother," Emily says. Emily's new family is doing what it can to ease her suffering. Her adoptive mother recently received permission from homeland security to bring Emily's youngest brother to the United States under a humanitarian parole. "I'm glad we are going to adopt my brother at Christmas—that will be the best day of my life. I think my mom will be glad that my brother and I will be together again. I want to forgive my mom, but I don't know how. It's hard to forgive someone that hurt you so bad."

Emily believes that her family could have stayed together and worked through the tough times, so she must deal with the difficult task of trying to accept her

World's Fastest Teen on Wheels

Tatyana McFadden was adopted from St. Petersburg, Russia, when she was six. Her adoptive mother, Deborah, went there to help start an adoption agency that would assist U.S. families in adopting physically handicapped children from Russia. Deborah was not looking to adopt when she embarked on this work trip, but she fell in love with Tatyana when she first laid eyes on her.

Tatyana was born with spina bifida, a defect in the neural tube that oc-curs during pregnancy. This birth defect caused her spinal column to not close completely as it normally would. As a result of her unprotected spinal cord, Tatyana became paralyzed from the waist down. As a young child, Tatyana was not given a wheelchair, so she crawled around the two-room orphanage on her hands. There were no toys in her stark institutional home either. Although this seventeen-year-old high school student cannot use her legs, Tatyana has become one of the world's fastest paraplegic track racers.

At the Paralympic Games in 2004, she won two medals. She completed the 100-meter dash in only 16.69 seconds. Her mother, Deborah, sometimes won-ders if Tatyana developed her incredible arm strength that allows her to push her chair at unbelievable speeds because she could only use her arms to move as a young child. It seems that Tatyana's early difficulties have actually helped her succeed in racing, the sport she loves. Tatyana enjoys competing and also plays hockey and basketball. She has found love, happiness, and a successful racing career in her American home in Maryland.[5]

birth mother's decision and make a new life for herself with her adoptive family. With the many complex problems Emily faces, she decided to seek the help of a trained counselor. Emily's adoptive mom, Carolyn, desperately wants to help her daughter find happiness and peace. Carolyn explains, "I have told my daughter that terrible things happened to her, and she needs to figure out how not to let what happened to her ruin the rest of her life."[4]

Foster Care

Unfortunately, some children are removed from their biological families by Child Protective Services or other government agencies. This delicate and often emotionally charged situation occurs when social workers determine that a child is being neglected or abused. For some children, leaving an abusive home can be an incredible relief, but for those who continue to feel a strong love and bonding with their birth parents despite the problems at home, emotions are mixed.

Children who are removed from their homes are often placed with foster care families with the hope their parents can be rehabilitated and eventually become responsible parents. While some children are able to return home to live with their parents, many do not. They may be shuttled between home and several different foster care families over a period of many years. In some of these cases, children end up finding a new home with an adoptive family. These children are given a fresh start, but are faced with fitting into an existing family and a new home.

Derrico's Story

Derrico had a rough life prior to his adoption, including physical abuse, bad foster care placements, and even a fire in the apartment where he lived. Through adoption, Derrico finally found a stable home and a second chance at life. Now in his

Foster Care in America

The U.S. Department of Health and Human Services reported that about 408,000 children were in the foster care system as of September 30, 2010. The average age of a child in the system was nine. Social workers set goals for each child based on their unique circumstances and family situation. The case goal for 51 percent of the children in foster care in 2010 was to reunite the child with his or her parents or original caretaker. In 25 percent of the cases the goal was to place the child in a new home through adoption. This translates to finding homes for approximately 102,000 children in foster care. Every year, many children move in and out of foster care. For example, 254,375 children entered foster care in 2010, while 254,114 left the system, with 52,340 of those children being adopted.[6]

twenties, he has a good job, is married, and has a darling two-year-old daughter who is the light of his life. Today, Derrico finds purpose and joy in helping other people, although there was little joy in his early years. Derrico shares his situation before he was adopted:

My birth mother was very young when I was born and then she had my little brother. She couldn't cope and got into drugs. My brother and I were put into the foster care system. By the time my adoptive mom saw our picture in a book of waiting kids, we'd been in seven foster homes. I was nine and my brother seven when we moved into our adoptive home. We became part of a family of seven kids.

Many of the foster families where Derrico stayed had good intentions, but unfortunately things didn't always work out. Later, Derrico's experiences in various foster care homes led to other issues as he grew older:

I think the biggest problem was lack of trust. Being in foster homes for years gave me time to learn not to trust anyone. I heard time and time again that I was loved and wanted, yet year after year, I saw my younger brother abused and us being yelled at and shipped around. So I became set in my ways, and thought to myself that I was grown already—that I had to

Derrico, his wife, Christia, and their daughter

take care of myself. To this day, I credit all that to foster care. I still don't trust a lot of people, and the word "love" has little meaning to me. It was tough being told you are loved and then see a foster family willingly let the agency send you off to another family. I went through that for years. Trust was taken from me a long time ago. My adoptive family did help me become more trusting. But it took time. At first, I was scared when my new mom drove me anywhere. I was sure she would have an accident or get lost. After awhile I began to relax and trust her.

Derrico was struggling with trust and other issues when he was adopted, but his new family helped him grow and move beyond some of his past. Derrico shares what his adoptive family means to him:

A lot of good has come from being adopted. I had the chance to have a family. I was raised in a good environment, and ended up meeting some good people. I'm now married with a child and doing well. I attribute that to my adoptive parents, who showed me the right way. Even if I chose another path, they pointed me in the right direction. I love my adoptive family. They didn't have to take me, but they did, and for that I am grateful to no end.

Although Derrico realizes that every adopted child's background is different, and their experiences as they move in with a new family will vary greatly, he also believes being adopted at an older age can be a positive experience if kids are willing to leave the past behind them and try to make things work with their adoptive family. Here's Derrico's advice for kids who are adopted when they are older: "Give your new parents a chance. They aren't perfect. Remember that you are now dealing with a whole different deck of cards. Give it time. Give yourself time."[7]

Staying in Touch with Birth and Adoptive Families

For some teens, a new adoptive family does not necessarily mean they will never see their birth family again. Such was the case with two teens, Olya and Anya, who were adopted from Russia. The two sisters were living at a children's home in Russia when they were adopted by a couple from California. The girls ended up in the home after their father died and their mother could not take care of them by herself. Although the sisters had several blood relatives in Russia, two grandmothers, an older half-brother, and an uncle, all of them were too poor to care for the girls.

After moving to California with their new adoptive family, Olya and Anya received phone calls and letters from their relatives asking for money. The girls wanted to help their Russian family members, so their new parents sent them some money. All would seem well for awhile, but then a different problem would arise and the family would ask for more money.

Olya and Anya felt caught in the middle. They were happy in their new home. They felt loved by their new adoptive family. The girls also enjoyed school and had made new friends, but they had many memories of their home in Russia. After five years in the United States, the sisters wanted to see their birth family and homeland.

In 2005, at the ages of fifteen and eighteen, Olya and Anya traveled back to Russia with their adoptive parents. It was a time of tears and joy. It was a time where two families, divided by thousands of miles, joined together for a short time as one. It was a time for Olya and Anya's new parents to understand the sacrifice their birth family had made in letting them go so that the girls would have opportunities that could lead to a better life. The visit was such a success for everyone that the sisters have been planning another trip back to Russia. Fortunately, these two girls have found a way to enjoy being part of a loving new family while still staying in close contact with their birth family.[8]

Kamal Finds a New Family

When Kamal's father moved from his home in Azerbaijan to take a job in another country, he left behind his young wife and their three children. Kamal's mother eventually found she could not feed and care for her children alone (women in Azerbaijan are not allowed to get jobs or earn their own money), so she placed them "temporarily" in an orphanage until things got better. But things apparently didn't get any better, because Kamal's mother never returned for them.

During their five years in the orphanage, Kamal and his younger brother and sister stuck together and looked out for each other. They helped each other get enough food and get along with the 167 other children in the facility. When Kamal became too old to stay in the orphanage, the staff there altered his birth date in their file. The caregivers wanted to make it appear that Kamal was younger than his true age in order to keep him from exceeding the age limit at the orphanage, which would have forced him to leave the facility and his two younger siblings. As a result of these altered documents, no one, including Kamal, knows how old he really is today.

When Kamal was around ten, he began a new chapter in his life. On December 24, 2003, Kamal and his siblings were adopted by a couple from the United States. The three only knew their native language of Azeri, but they quickly

> ## It's a Fact!
>
> Azerbaijan is in the southwestern part of Asia. It is located between Iran and Russia, with part of its shore along the Caspian Sea. This small country is slightly smaller than the state of Maine and is home to about 8 million people. Azerbaijan gained its independence from the Soviet Union in 1991. As a new country, Azerbaijan initially enjoyed eighteen months of peace before war broke out.[9]

learned the English language their new parents spoke. This family of five first lived in China, where Kamal's adoptive parents were staying during a two-year work assignment.

After Kamal's adoptive father finished his job in China, the family moved to a suburb of Chicago. As Kamal settled into the United States, he faced many new and challenging situations. He experienced significant culture shock, as he was bombarded by America's incessant and powerful media. He was unprepared to take in the consumeristic and provocative messages from music, advertisements, and television. Kamal was accustomed to having only one television channel to view on the single TV set in the orphanage, which worked only when it had electricity. One of his fondest memories while living in the orphanage was watching Tom and Jerry cartoons.

When Kamal began attending middle school in the United States, he was unsure how to interact with other teens. He had much to learn about typical teen behavior, including how teens dress, talk, and even what they eat. One stumbling block for Kamal was his dark hair, brown eyes, and olive-colored skin, and the assumptions others made about his nationality based solely on his appearance. Uninformed and narrow-minded teens drew conclusions about him, based on their false assumptions of his race. Prejudice is always an ugly thing, no matter where, when, or to whom it is directed. While facing difficulties at school, Kamal found that his love of sports, soccer, basketball, and wrestling helped him find areas of common ground where he could relate to other kids. Kamal was academically behind the other students in his grade, but he worked very hard in his studies to catch up. Since his exact age was unknown, it was hard for the school to know the appropriate grade where he should be placed. As Kamal faced struggles both socially and academically, it was difficult for him to ask for help. At times, he was afraid to voice his fears or share what he didn't know.

Along with his challenges at school, Kamal was also still discovering his role in his new adoptive family. He was learning what it meant to have two parents who love him and how to cooperate with their authority. During his first year in the United States, Kamal and his parents disagreed about the importance of schoolwork. Part of that conflict was due to the fact that in Kamal's native country, Azerbaijan, learning a trade or a useful skill is deemed much more important than academic studies. As time passed, Kamal began to understand the value of education in the United States. He greatly improved his grades in his second year at middle school in 2006, and has dreams of attending college. Kamal loves cars and dreams of pursuing a career in that field, or in the area of robotics.

Even though Kamal endured many difficulties in his life, through those trials he has gained many positive qualities. Kamal has a strong sense of empathy toward others. He appreciates the comforts of his home and the gift of leisure, things most teens take for granted. Kamal has a kind spirit and is very generous. Past troubles have given Kamal great inner strength, which will be invaluable as he pursues his goals in the future.[10]

A New Dad and a New Family

Hope was two years old when her father passed away. She doesn't have any memories of him, only those that others have shared with her. When Hope was six, her mother remarried. Hope's "new" dad adopted her the following year. Now a teen, Hope reflects on the feelings she had when she was adopted at the age of seven, and discusses some issues she now faces as a teen:

I was six when my mom married Stuart. I remember how excited I was to finally have a dad. I had always wanted someone I could call "Dad." I couldn't remember my real father. The hardest part about getting a new dad was sharing Mom. Before Stuart came along, I did everything with Mom—shopping, going to the movies, reading books together, and playing games. I even slept in her room. When Mom first became serious with Stuart, I got scared that she would forget about me. It felt strange when they went out on a date and left me behind. But I had to learn that it was OK for her to love someone else. I was also happy they were dating, because I could see how happy Mom was. Before Stuart came along, sometimes life was difficult for just the two of us. Stuart was very sweet and helped us a lot.

After my mom got married and Stuart adopted me, things seemed to change so fast. And those changes were hard! I began to wonder if *everything* was going to completely change. First, we moved in with Dad. Lots of things around the house changed too. Simple things we had not thought about before, such as choosing a family activity. We had to find something that *everyone* wanted to do. Before, when it was just Mom and I, she was very flexible and we usually did whatever I wanted. Also, Dad had more rules than Mom. He was the rule setter in the house, and it took some time for me to understand why he set certain boundaries. After awhile, I thought about the fact that I was his first and only child and that he was just being protective. As I look back at all my dad has done for me, I realize I am very fortunate to have a dad who looks out for me the way he does.

Now that I'm older, I am facing different kinds of problems. Many of them have to do with my dad's last name—Nishimoto. I took his name when he adopted me. Some kids ask, "Are you Japanese?" It's tough when people give me weird looks and say things like, "You have blue eyes and brown hair. How can your name be Nishimoto?" Bolder people have asked if my parents are divorced and other tough questions. Sometimes when I get really mad and frustrated at Dad, I'm tempted to blurt out, "You're not my real dad." But I'm learning that anger is not a good reason to hurt him. He has helped guide me through some tough times over the years. My friends wonder why I call him Dad, but I explain that's what he has always been to me. He's parented me for a long time and I love him very much.[11]

Blending Families

Sometimes single parents remarry, thus creating one new family by merging their two separate families together. In some "blended" families, the children will be formally adopted by their parent's new spouse. This may occur when the child's original birth parent is no longer a part of their life, due to an untimely death, abandonment, or perhaps when a parent is sent to jail. When a new parent is suddenly added to your life (and possibly new siblings), this can bring about major changes in your life. These changes can be exciting, wonderful, and stressful all at the same time.

All Part of the Family

No matter how you became part of your new family, and regardless of how wonderful your family is, you probably still have some concerns and difficulties. Below is a list of suggestions that can help you open up, share your concerns, and discover ways to adapt to your family situation. Hopefully some of these ideas will help make the transition into your adoptive family a little easier:

- Voice your concerns or problems as you fit into your new family. Don't bottle up your feelings.

- Take time to grieve the loss of the mother, father, or caregiver that is no longer in your life. Unexpressed pain or sadness can negatively affect your relationship with the new adoptive parents in your life.
- Write a letter to a birth parent, even if you don't have an address to mail it to. It could provide an outlet for your pent-up feelings. Writing out your thoughts may allow you to identify what exactly you are truly struggling with, and perhaps the reasons behind those struggles.
- Spend some special time with your new parent by yourself. Go to a concert or sporting event together. Remember—forming a new parental bond takes time.
- While keeping old traditions is important, it's also key that you create some new family rituals with your adoptive parents.
- Keep a realistic perspective. Realize that all people have their faults and shortcomings. Don't expect your new parents to be perfect. Allow them to make a few mistakes, but remember to share those things that are really bothering you.

What about You?

There are many different reasons older children end up being adopted and becoming part of a new family. Although each adopted child has his or her own unique past, many face some of the same issues in their lives after being adopted. Emotions such as rejection, guilt, anger, and sadness are common struggles for those adopted when they are older. This mixed bag of unresolved feelings can disrupt their daily lives and keep them from enjoying the good things in their lives today.

Do you ever feel like you are carrying around excess emotional baggage due to your adoption? Does it sometimes seem like there is a battle going on between your head and your heart? Do you find yourself going over your past to understand the reasons why your birth mother or father chose adoption for you, only to discover that no matter how compelling these facts may be, they don't erase the pain and loss in your heart? Make sure you share those feelings with an adoptive parent, a trusted friend, or a counselor. Don't keep them pent up and allow them to hurt your current relationships.

You may also feel torn between your old family and your new one—perhaps even disloyal or guilty as you begin to bond with your new adoptive family. It may seem that you are giving the love that rightly belongs to your biological parents to your adoptive parents. If you have experienced these feelings, rest assured that you have plenty of love for all your parents and new family members. You can share a unique love and lasting bond with your birth parents and an equally special love with your adoptive parents.

Discussion Questions

What do you think changed the most after you were adopted?

How has your new family helped you?

If you could send a message to anyone in the world, who would you send it to and what would it be?

How can dwelling on the past be helpful or hurtful?

What are some of your goals for the future?

What are a few easy first steps you could take to start working toward those goals?

Notes

1. Emily, e-mail correspondence, August 8, 2006.
2. "Length of Orphanage Stay Matters," *Adoptive Families* (June 2006), 11.
3. Fernanda Santos, "Painful Reality TV," *New York Times*, December 9, 2005, B1.
4. Carolyn and Emily, e-mail correspondence, August 8, 2006.
5. Baltimore Sun, "Tatyana McFadden, Wheelchair Racing," www.baltimoresun.com/sports/olympics/bal-oly-mcfadden,0,6844772.storygallery (accessed December 14, 2006).
6. U.S. Department of Health and Human Services, Children's Bureau, "The AFCARS Report—Preliminary FY 2010 Estimates as of June 2011 (18)," n.d., www.acf.hhs.gov/programs/cb/stats_research/afcars/tar/report18.htm (accessed March 28, 2012).
7. Derrico, e-mail correspondence, October 9, 2006.
8. Meredith Resnick, "My Turn: We Didn't Need the Past—Or So I Thought," *Newsweek*, www.msnbc.msn.com/id/13528589/site/newsweek (accessed August 2, 2006).
9. World Factbook, "Azerbaijan Geography," education.yahoo.com/reference/factbook/aj/geogra.html;_ylt=AnNOXBZNkSfXbn127bmQZSq4ecYF (accessed August 13, 2006).
10. Margaret (Kamal's adoptive mother), author interview, December 13, 2006.
11. Hope, telephone interview, October 23, 2006.

A REAL FAMILY

··

"My family feels completely 'real' to me due to the fact that it is real. My parents and my sister have raised me well before I had any capacity for memory. All I've ever known was them. They socialized me, fed me, taught me, and have always been my family in all aspects."[1]—Billy, age 19

The introduction of this book provided Webster's definition of real—something that is authentic and genuine. So what is a real family? Obviously every person has his or her own definition of what comprises an authentic or genuine family.

Redefining Family

In today's world, the combination of people that make up a family is constantly changing. For some, a single mother and her baby form a family. A dad and two teens may make up another family. Recently, many grandparents have taken on the responsibility of raising their grandchildren, resulting in yet another type of family. When couples with children divorce and remarry, new, blended families are created. Adoptive families come together in innumerable ways. Some contain members who belong to different races. Many adopted teens have folded their birth family members into their adoptive family, creating one large extended family. In some open adoptions, a birth parent has a relationship with his or her biological child that is similar to a close relative, like a favorite aunt or uncle. Perhaps this brief discussion of the different ways a family can form will remind you that a couple and their biological children is only one of the many possible combinations that result in a family.

For many teens, their adoptive family is very real to them. They believe the parents who have loved and cared for them through good times and bad are nothing less than the real deal. The brothers and sisters in their family, the ones they have fought with, laughed with, shared with, and cried with, are also an authentic part of their real family.

Off the Bookshelf

Adoption Nation: How the Adoption Revolution Is Transforming America is a powerfully written book that examines the major impact adoption has had in the United States. The author, Adam Pertman, is the father of two privately adopted children. Both of these adoptions were later opened. In his book, Pertman discusses many topics of interest to teens such as access to birth records, legal issues adoptees face, ethics in adoption, and the newest findings on the benefits of open adoptions. *Adoption Nation* takes an honest look at the current attitudes, as well as past ideals and beliefs, about adoption. This insightful book can help you put your adoption experiences, both affirming and challenging, into perspective as you reflect on how adoption fits in your life. A major theme throughout the text is that society needs to become better educated about adoption and recognize that adopted children are no different from other members of a family—cherished, important, valuable, and loved. *Adoption Nation* was first published in 2000 and an updated edition was released in 2011.

Where's the Happy Ending?

While it would be nice to paint the rosy picture that all adopted teens are completely happy with their adoption situation and new family, unfortunately this isn't always the case. Some teens may struggle with feelings that their adoptive family does not seem like a real family to them. They may experience differences with other family members that cast a dark, negative light on the family as a whole. Relationships that are difficult during certain times in a person's life can become completely different in later years. For some, differences and negative feelings subside or disappear all together as the people involved become older and more mature.

Another situation that can cause a teen to wish for a more "normal" or "real" home life is when one member of a family is battling a major issue, such as alcoholism, drug abuse, or a serious illness. The relational strife caused by these circumstances can seem too big to overcome and can disrupt the function of the entire family unit. Counseling or other outside help can give teens the assistance they need to work through most difficult issues within the family. Unfortunately, not every major concern is always resolved, and some adopted teens may not find what they consider to be a "real" family until they start one of their own someday.

Holidays Bring out Buried Emotions

Holidays are often a time of relaxation and celebrating with your family. However, certain holidays, such as Mother's Day or Father's Day, can be stressful for adopted teens. Some teens experience mixed feelings on these days that range from joy, thankfulness, and appreciation to loss, sorrow, or guilt. They may feel grateful for the adoptive parents who have loved and raised them, yet at the same time feel sad that they do not know their birth parents or even if they are all right. Birthdays can be another time when adopted teens face confusing emotions. Of course it's a day to celebrate, eat cake, and rake in the presents, but for some teens it may serve as a reminder that their birth parents chose not to keep them and cause them once again to wonder why.

What's Real to You?

Many teens, adopted or not, face difficult times when the relationships in their families are strained, difficult, or seemingly impossible. Let's face it—most of us have a few family members we wouldn't mind trading in for an "improved model." We watch the wonderful families in sitcom shows that laugh their way through difficulties and end up solving all their problems in a half-hour episode, and wonder why we didn't get a family like that. This thought can sometimes lead people to wish they belonged to a better or different family, rather than their flawed or seemingly dysfunctional one. Everyone daydreams at times, but for some adopted teens, this could lead to unrealistic fantasies about their birth

> **Abuse Is Not Okay**
>
> This chapter discusses the fact that every family will experience times when some members do not get along and suggests ways to "hang in there" and improve these relationships. If you feel there is emotional or physical abuse in your family, talk to a trusted adult, teacher, or school counselor about it. Get some outside help. Abuse in any type of family should not be tolerated and is never okay.

families. Have you ever been tempted to believe that your life would be perfect if you lived with your birth family? If you dwell on these idealistic thoughts for too long, it can become misleading and destructive. You may decide to not put any effort into the relationships with your family because it's not your biological, or "real," family anyway. In all families, everyone needs to keep trying to make things better. Family members need to forgive, help, share, laugh, encourage, and love, even when they don't feel like it. Don't give up on your family—they will never give up on you.

Real to Me

In the end, you are the only one who will know what a real family means to you. You decide what makes it real. Is it size? Color of skin? Genes? Unconditional love? It's hard to say just what particular components come together to form a family. Perhaps it's the fact that you help each other through good times and bad. One of the amazing things about a family is that its members can be so different, yet so closely connected at the same time.

The good news is that thousands of teens who have been adopted feel that their adoptive family is not only real, but that it is the only family they can imagine being a part of. Alana is an African American eighteen-year-old who lives in California. She was adopted when she was a baby by her Caucasian parents. Her older adopted brother is also African American. She shares her feelings about her perception of family, "Why wouldn't my adoptive parents feel like a real family to me? They raised me, changed my diapers. They taught me to speak, to walk, to be who I am, and be proud of that. They're the only kind of family I know, so they are most definitely 'real' to me. They mean everything to me. I love them."[2]

Consider Becoming a Mentor

As a teen, you have the opportunity to help younger adopted kids as they encounter adoption-related issues that you may have already worked through. If you enjoy being around younger kids, becoming a mentor to an adopted child may be very rewarding and worthwhile for you. As a mentor, you can share some of your own adoption experiences and help them with their concerns. Acting as a "big brother" or "big sister," you can be a significant source of help to kids by simply giving them a set of ears that are eager to listen. You may be able to relate to them and help in a way that their parents or other adults can't.

Many adoption agencies and adoption support organizations have recently started mentoring programs. If you want to get involved helping younger kids, contact an adoption agency or adoptee support group in your area. For more information about mentoring, check out the National Mentoring Partnership website at www.mentoring.org. There you will find basic information about becoming a mentor, along with personal stories of how mentors have changed kids' lives.

One story on the Mentoring Partnership website tells of a young boy, David, who was born in the Phillipines and adopted when he was young by a couple living in New York. Later, David started attending public school and found there were very few Asian American students. He struggled to develop relationships with other kids and began having trouble relating to his Jewish parents. His mother contacted the Asian Professional Extension (APEX), which paired David with an Asian American mentor named Wilson. The two quickly bonded and found they had a lot in common. Wilson helped David connect with his cultural heritage, tutored him in schoolwork, and was a real source of strength when David's parents later divorced. Wilson has played an invaluable role in David's life as his mentor.[3]

"When I went to Korea for the first time, I was forced to confront my own adoption. No longer could I pretend that I was not adopted. One of the reasons I delayed going to Korea was my fear of how my adoptive parents would feel. I feared that if I met my birth family, the only parents I knew might feel I did not love them. I did not want my reunion with my birth family to negate the years of nurture given to me by my adoptive parents.

"On the night before I left for Korea, I sat with my parents on our back patio, my fears locked in my heart. Then my dad dispelled my worries by saying, 'We always knew we had family in Korea.' They accepted my Korean family as they had accepted me twenty-one years ago. They felt no competition for my love."[4]—Hollee McGinnis, Policy and Operations Director, Evan B. Donaldson Adoption Institute

Bryant

Bryant, age nineteen, explains how his birth and adoptive families have combined to form his unique and very real family:

My birth mom, Allison, gave birth to me. She cares about me and I care about her. I have known her my entire life. She is like family to me. I have visited her and she has come to visit us. When I went to see her, we did kid stuff because she has kids and they are my little sisters. Allison's husband is like a stepdad to me, a buddy. My mom and dad take me to see my birth mother and have always included her in our family. The family I grew up in is like a bunch of families, but I consider it one family and I am thankful for having so many people that love me.[5]

A Poem Written by Billy, Age 19, about His Adoptive Father, Bill

Hero
I look to my hero
As the waves look to the moon
For direction

Billy and his father, Bill

I look to my hero
As the beggar looks to the people walking by
For help

I look to my hero
As Galileo looked to the sky
For knowledge

And for everything
I owe him the world he gave me

And through everything
I never want to hurt him
Though I do

And through everything
I never want to lose him
Though I will

But he won't leave me
And I won't leave him
He was there from the beginning
I'll be there to the end

Maybe I'll be my son's hero
And he'll look to me
And I'll never fail
As mine never did
And I'll look to mine
To know what a hero really is

If I'm half the man my father was
I'll be the second greatest man to ever live.

Looking up to
Listening to
Talking to
My hero

My father

This art, drawn by a birth mother named Mary, depicts all three parts of an adoption as people traveling the same road through life. They may take different paths, but they have the same destination of eternity with God together.

> "Many adoptees have told me that after meeting their birth family, they realized their 'real' parents were the ones who adopted them."—Hollee McGinnis, Policy and Operations Director, Evan B. Donaldson Adoption Institute

What about You?

Your adoptive family can be an authentic and genuine family, no matter how it was created. No doubt, it will have some flaws, like all families. And these will probably include some of the common teen complaints such as nagging parents, annoying siblings, and unfair rules. But if you look around, you'll soon discover that these same issues plague most families. Just remember—every family is different and is created in its own unique way. Every family shares its own special experiences and creates its own memories. So enjoy your family members for who they are—not perfect, but your family just the same.

Discussion Questions

How do you define a "family"?

What can you do to help make your family better?

How do the other members of your family help you?

What do you like most about your family?

Notes

1. Billy, e-mail correspondence, April 10, 2006.
2. Alanna, e-mail correspondence, March 10, 2006.
3. MENTOR, "Wilson and David—Brooklyn, New York," www.mentoring.org/mentoring_month/meet_mentors_mentees/wilson_and_david.php (accessed September 26, 2006).
4. Hollee McGinnis, e-mail correspondence, December 5, 2006.
5. Bryant, e-mail correspondence, April 5, 2006.

Glossary

birth family any biological family member of a child who is placed for adoption

birth mother a woman who gives birth to a child and places him or her for adoption

birth parent a biological parent

closed adoption an adoption in which the identities and contact information of the adopted person and birth family are never shared; sometimes referred to as a confidential adoption

domestic adoption when a child is adopted by a family that lives in the same country where the child was born

international adoption when a family that is living in one country adopts a child who is born and currently living in another country

nonidentifying information information about a person that does not reveal the person's identity

open adoption an adoption agreement where some type of openness or sharing of information exists. The birth family and adoptive family often determine the type and amount of information that is shared, and if and how much contact there will be between the adopted person and the birth family.

parental rights a parent's rights to take proper care of a child, both physically and emotionally, as well as make a myriad of decisions that will affect a child

private adoption when a child is adopted by a nonrelative without the assistance of an adoption agency

putative father a person who professes or is alleged to be the father of a child born out of wedlock (even if there is not sufficient evidence at the time to prove this allegation is true). Most states have a putative father registry where a man who believes he has fathered a child with a woman he is not married to may register, and in doing so, claim he is the father of this child.

semi-open adoption a type of adoption that maintains the privacy of all parties involved, while still allowing contact through a third party such as an agency or attorney. Generally, addresses and phone numbers are not shared, but first names and other nonidentifying information is exchanged.

statutes laws

traditional adoption another term for closed adoption

transracial adoption   when a child is adopted by a family of a different race

triad   a term commonly used to mean the three parties involved in an adoption, including the birth family, the child placed for adoption, and the adoptive family

For Further Information

General Adoption Resources

About Adoption—Resources on Adoption
www.adoption.com
 Information on adoption and reunion for birth parents, adoptive parents, foster parents, and adoptees.

Adoption/Foster Care
www.adoption.about.com
 Basic information about adoption and links to many adoption articles.

Adoption Clubhouse
www.adoptionclubhouse.org

Adoption History Project
www.uoregon.edu/~adoption/topics/index.html
 Contains information about the history of adoption and adoption statistics.

Adoption Learning Partners
www.AdoptionLearningPartners.org
 Provides valuable and up-to-date educational resources for adoptive parents, adopted individuals, birth parents, and the families that love them.

***Adoption Today* magazine**
www.adoptinfo.net
 Review articles regarding adoption, foster care, and some articles from back issues. Also contains subscription information and resources.

Adoption.org
www.adoption.org
 An extensive database of adoption resources.

***Adoptive Families* magazine**
www.adoptivefamilies.com
 National adoption magazine for families before, during, and after adoption.

American Adoption Congress
www.americanadoptioncongress.org
PO Box 42730
Washington, D.C. 20015
(202) 483-3399

Center for Adoption Support and Education
www.adoptionsupport.org
National resource for families and professionals, providing training, publications, and consultation.

Center for Family Connections
www.kinnect.org
Nationwide consultation and professional peer network.

Child Welfare Information Gateway
www.childwelfare.gov/adoption/index.cfm
Provides resources on all aspects of domestic and intercountry adoption, including adoption from foster care. Includes information about searching for birth relatives, types of adoptions, adoption support groups, and postadoption services. It's full of great stuff! Printable factsheets on adoption available at:

- Impact of Adoption on Adopted Persons: www.childwelfare.gov/pubs/f_adimpact.cfm
- Parenting the Adopted Adolescent: www.childwelfare.gov/pubs/f_adoles/index.cfm
- Adoption and the Stages of Development: www.childwelfare.gov/pubs/f_stages/index.cfm
- After Adoption: The Need for Services: www.childwelfare.gov/pubs/f_after/index.cfm
- Adoption and School Issues: www.childwelfare.gov/pubs/f_school/index.cfm

Child Welfare League of America
www.cwla.org

ComeUnity
www.comeunity.com
A website devoted to providing resources on parenting, adoption, and children's special needs. This site contains articles, e-mail directories for many countries, expert interviews, and book reviews.

Concerned United Birthparents
www.cubirthparents.org

The Dave Thomas Foundation for Adoption
www.davethomasfoundation.org

Evan B. Donaldson Adoption Institute
www.adoptioninstitute.org

Families Adopting in Response
www.fairfamilies.org

Volunteer organization that supports, educates, and advocates for adoptive families. Publishes *Adoption and the Schools: Resources for Parents and Teachers.*

Hand in Hand
www.handinhandparenting.org

Helps parents acquire the skills they need to build and rebuild close connections with their children. Encourages parents to build close connections with other parents so that they are able to learn and share with others and work together to build a healthier community.

Insight: Open Adoption Resources and Support
www.openadoptioninsight.org

Let's Talk Adoption
www.letstalkadoption.com/index.html

The website home of a radio show featuring various adoption topics hosted by Mardie Caldwell. Previous shows can be accessed through this website.

National Adoption Center
www.adopt.org

National Council for Adoption
www.adoptioncouncil.org

National Foster Care and Adoption Directory Search
www.childwelfare.gov:80/nfcad

The National Foster Care and Adoption Directory (formerly the National Adoption Directory) offers a state-by-state listing of adoption and foster care resources.

North American Council on Adoptable Children

www.nacac.org

A national organization founded by adoptive parents, NACAC advocates the right of every child to a permanent, continuous, nurturing, and culturally sensitive family, and presses for the legal adoptive placement of any child denied that right.

Transracial and International Adoption

Colorado Heritage Camps

www.heritagecamps.org

A postadoption resource that facilitates annual heritage camps, which provide culturally relevant and family-centered experiences for every member of the family. Camps representing a variety of cultures are held each summer.

Families for Russian and Ukrainian Adoption (FRUA)

www.frua.org

With chapters across the United States and members around the world, FRUA provides international adoption support resources for families completed through adoption in Eastern European and Central Asian countries.

Families with Cambodian Children

www.famcam.org

Families with Children from China (FCC)

www.fwcc.org

Filipino Adoptees Network

www.filipino-adoptees-network.org

Korean American Adoptee Adoptive Family Network (KAAN)

www.kaanet.com

KAAN links Korean adoptive families and adoptees, the Korean American community, and the Korean government to promote awareness of Korean adoption issues, resource sharing, information, and program development.

Korean Focus

koreanfocus.org

Pact, An Adoption Alliance

www.pactadopt.org

Pact believes that in making an adoption plan, birth parents and adoptive parents enter into an agreement to recognize and protect the best interests of the child. Essential to that agreement is a lifelong commitment to recognize, respect, and address the dual heritages—both personal and cultural—that are the child's birthright. Pact's goal is for every child to feel wanted, honored, and loved, a cherished member of a strong family with a proud connection to his or her rich heritage.

Adopted Vietnamese International (AVI)

www.adoptedvietnamese.org

AVI is a volunteer network that is dedicated to Vietnamese adoptees who were adopted before, during, or in connection with the Vietnam War.

Search and Reunion

Adoption Search Engine

www.adoptionsearch.com

Helps you search the web for adoption-related content.

The International Soundex Reunion Registry

www.ISRR.org

A nonprofit, tax exempt, humanitarian agency founded in 1975 by Emma May Vilardi. ISRR is a mutual consent reunion registry for persons desiring a reunion with next of kin.

Metro Reunion Registry

www.MetroReunionRegistry.org

Free registry to help reunite adoptees with birth families.

National Listing of Adoption Search and Support Groups

www.paadoptionreunionregistry.org

The White Oak Foundation

www.whiteoakfoundation.org/mappage.htm

Information about U.S. adoption statutes.

Organizations

American Adoption Congress

www.americanadoptioncongress.org

PO Box 42730
Washington, D.C. 20015
(202) 483-3399

Concerned United Birthparents
www.cubirthparents.org

Child Welfare League of America
www.cwla.org

The Dave Thomas Foundation for Adoption
www.davethomasfoundation.org
716 Mt. Airyshire Blvd., Suite 100
Columbus, OH 43235
1-800-ASK-DTFA (1-800-275-3832)

Evan B. Donaldson Adoption Institute
www.adoptioninstitute.org

Center for Adoption Support and Education
www.adoptionsupport.org
    National resource for families and professionals, providing training, publications, and consultation.

Center for Family Connections: www.kinnect.org
    Nationwide consultation and professional peer network.

Families Adopting in Response
www.fairfamilies.org
    Volunteer organization that supports, educates, and advocates for adoptive families.

The International Re-evaluation Counseling Communities
719 Second Ave. N.
Seattle, WA 98109
(206) 284-0311
promotes peer counseling and information on "special time" playing.

North American Council on Adoptable Children
www.nacac.org

A national organization founded by adoptive parents in 1974, NACAC promotes and supports permanent families for children and youth in the United States and Canada who have been in care—especially those in foster care and those with special needs.

Suggested Reading

Bailey, Julie Jarrell, and Lynn N. Giddens. *The Adoption Reunion Survival Guide: Preparing Yourself For the Search, Reunion, and Beyond*. Oakland, CA: New Harbinger Publications, Inc., 2001.

Brodzinsky, David M., and Marshall D. Schechter, eds. *The Psychology of Adoption*. New York: Oxford University Press, 1990.

Brodzinksy, David M., Marshall D. Schechter, and Robin Marantz Henig. *Being Adopted: The Lifelong Search For Self*. New York: Doubleday, 1992.

Cohen, Shari. *Coping With Being Adopted*. New York: Rosen Publishing Group, 1998.

Eldridge, Sherrie. *Twenty Life-Transforming Choices Adoptees Need to Make*. Colorado Springs, CO: Pinon Press, 2003.

Kaminker, Laura. *Everything You Need to Know About Being Adopted*. New York: Rosen Publishing, 1999.

McColm, Michelle. *Adoption Reunions: A Book For Adoptees, Birth Parents and Adoptive Families*. Toronto: Second Story Press, 1993.

Pertman, Adam. *Adoption Nation: How the Adoption Revolution is Transforming America*. New York: Basic Books, 2006.

Robinson, Katy. *A Single Square Picture*. New York: Berkeley Publishing Group, 2002.

Steinberg, Gail, and Beth Hall. *Inside Transracial Adoption*. Indianapolis, IN: Perspectives Press, 2000.

Strauss, Jean A.S. *Birthright: The Guide to Search and Reunion for Adoptees, Birthparents, and Adoptive Parents*. New York: Penguin Books, 1994.

Weiss, Ann E. *Adoptions Today: Questions and Controversies*. Brookfield, CT: Millbrook Press, 2001.

Index

About the Author and Photographer

Suzanne Buckingham Slade is the author of more than ninety books for children and young adults. Her works include picture books, biographies, books on various science topics, outdoor sports, astronomy, and nature, and Bible storybooks. Ms. Slade holds a Bachelor of Science in Mechanical Engineering and worked in the engineering field for several years before beginning her writing career. Originally from Goshen, Indiana, she now lives outside Chicago with her husband, Mike, and two children, Christina and Patrick. Ms. Slade is an adoptive mother and has a passion for encouraging adopted children and families. She has also written on the topic of adoption for *Adoptive Families* magazine. You can learn more about Suzanne Slade on her website, www.suzanneslade.com.

Chris Washburn is a freelance photographer who resides in a northern suburb of Chicago. Mr. Washburn provided four photos for the cover and his work also appears in this book. His portfolio can be viewed at www.geocities.com/christopher .washburn.